THE COMPLETE BOOK OF
DECORATIVE
STENCILING

THE COMPLETE BOOK OF

DECORATIVE STENCILING

A complete manual
featuring 75 projects and
over 800 photographs

How to decorate and
personalize your home
with beautiful stencils

LUCINDA
GANDERTON

This edition is published by Lorenz Books

Lorenz Books is an imprint of Anness Publishing Ltd
Hermes House, 88–89 Blackfriars Road, London SE1 8HA
tel. 020 7401 2077; fax 020 7633 9499
www.lorenzbooks.com; info@anness.com

© Anness Publishing Ltd 2005

UK agent: The Manning Partnership Ltd, 6 The Old Dairy, Melcombe Road, Bath BA2 3LR;
tel. 01225 478444; fax 01225 478440; sales@manning-partnership.co.uk

UK distributor: Grantham Book Services Ltd, Isaac Newton Way, Alma Park Industrial Estate, Grantham, Lincs NG31 9SD;
tel. 01476 541080; fax 01476 541061; orders@gbs.tbs-ltd.co.uk

North American agent/distributor: National Book Network, 4501 Forbes Boulevard, Suite 200, Lanham, MD 20706;
tel. 301 459 3366; fax 301 429 5746; www.nbnbooks.com

Australian agent/distributor: Pan Macmillan Australia, Level 18, St Martins Tower, 31 Market St, Sydney, NSW 2000;
tel. 1300 135 113; fax 1300 135 103; customer.service@macmillan.com.au

New Zealand agent/distributor: David Bateman Ltd, 30 Tarndale Grove, Off Bush Road, Albany, Auckland;
tel. (09) 415 7664; fax (09) 415 8892

A CIP catalogue record for this book is available from the British Library.

Publisher: Joanna Lorenz
Editorial director: Judith Simons
Senior editor: Doreen Gillon
Editor: Judy Cox
Additional text: Petra Boase, Emma Hardy, Sacha Cohen, Alison Jenkins,
Cheryl Owen, Liz Wagstaff, Stewart and Sally Walton
Special photography: Paul Bricknell, with additional photography by Tim Imrie,
Debbie Patterson, Graham Rae, Steve Tanner, Adrian Taylor
Stylist for special photography: Tamsin Weston
Designer: Bill Mason
Production controller: Stephen Lang
Editorial reader: Jay Thundercliffe

1 3 5 7 9 10 8 6 4 2

Publisher's note
The authors and publisher have made every effort to ensure that all the instructions contained in this book are
accurate and that the safest methods are recommended. Readers should follow all recommended safety procedures
and wear protective goggles, gloves and clothing when necessary and work in a well-ventilated area. You should
know how to use your tools and equipment safely and make sure you are confident about what you are doing.
The publisher and authors cannot accept liability for any injury, damage or loss to persons or property as a result
of using any equipment in this book or carrying out any of the projects.

CONTENTS

INTRODUCTION

Stencilling is an enduringly popular art form, which is as fashionable now as it has been for many centuries. Versatile and adaptable, it has evolved alongside changing tastes in interior decoration, from Victorian Gothic to Bloomsbury bohemian, and new techniques and images are constantly being developed to fit in with current styles. After a decade of minimalism and plain walls, colour and pattern are once again finding their way back into our homes and interiors, and today's designers are once again reinterpreting traditional stencilling in an exciting new way. The most up-to-date stencils are both bold in design and colour and they are graphic, with an unmistakably 21st-century look.

SIMPLE STENCILS

Stencilling is straightforward, easy to put into practice and above all, great fun to do. The beauty of it, and much of the reason for its continued popularity, is that you can achieve professional-looking results very quickly and easily, without having any previous experience. There is great satisfaction in peeling back a stencil to reveal a crisply detailed one-off image, and also in building up a pattern or border from a repeated motif.

Any surface that can be painted can be stencilled using the wide range of specialist paints available from craft suppliers and art stores. From tiles, glass and plaster to fabric, paper and wood, the choices are endless and there is great scope for creativity. Depending on your own tastes, your time and your patience, you can decorate anything from an entire room, a table or a curtain to a greetings card or confetti box.

USING THIS BOOK

This book is a comprehensive guide to the techniques and an invaluable resource for everybody who is interested in stencilling, from the complete novice to the experienced crafter. The practical introduction covers everything you will need to know about cutting a stencil from card or plastic, and the different methods of applying colour by brush, roller or sponge to create various painted effects. There is a fascinating survey of historic stencilling styles, many of which are reflected in the projects, together with basic lessons in pattern making. The following chapters show you how to put all this information into practice and illustrate the vast potential of stencilled ornament in modern design and interior decoration. The inspirational ideas range from sheets of wrapping paper that can quickly be finished in an afternoon to entire room schemes that may take weeks to complete. Under chapter headings from "Walls and Surfaces" and "Furniture and Storage" to "Fabrics" and "Home Accessories" you will find a wealth of ideas to make for your home and as gifts for your friends and family.

None of these need be costly, particularly at a time when salvage and recycling are key trends. Much early American folk-art stencilling was a thrifty way of recreating the wallpaper and rugs that were prohibitively expensive in the New World, and a stencilled design on sanded boards or a painted floor cloth is still a very stylish alternative to a carpet. Most of us have a slightly shabby piece of furniture, tucked away in a spare room, that can be revamped with a fresh coat of paint and a few stencils, or a plain throw or bedcover that can be given a new lease of life with a scattering of stencilled motifs.

GETTING STARTED

Stencilling does not require much outlay of time or money. You may have some of the basic tools and art materials around the house and acrylic paints are relatively

OPPOSITE TOP: This rose-covered tree makes a bold feature on a pastel wall.

OPPOSITE BELOW: Classic motifs are ideal for a continuous floor border.

RIGHT: Faux stencilled shelves enliven any kitchen alcove.

inexpensive. New innovations such as the heat pen and easy-to-cut acetate have speeded up the process of making stencils from the days when they were hand cut from sheet metal, and photocopying saves a lot of time. Once you have chosen and made your first stencil, spend a little time experimenting with paint techniques and develop a few ideas of your own. All the

projects have detailed instructions, which are fully illustrated with step-by-step photographs: you can follow these to the letter or use your own imagination to interpret the designs as you wish. Whatever the results, your stencilled creations will always be quite unique, as no two people will ever interpret a project in the same way.

STENCILLING STYLES

The sheer versatility of stencilling means that it has appeared in many different guises over the years, and historic stencilling ranges from the purely functional to the highly decorative. Reverse stencil hand prints have been found in prehistoric cave dwellings, Egyptian tombs had stencilled patterning and Japanese fabrics were stencilled with "katagami" – resist floral designs. In the 1920s Mariano Fortuny recreated renaissance patterns on stencilled velvet and embellished them with Venetian glass beads. In more recent times it was even used as a propaganda medium by Italian fascists and Basque separatists, and hijacked by graffiti artists in both Europe and America, whose paintings have developed into popular street art.

PRACTICAL STENCILLING

Today stencilling is thought of as a purely decorative craft, but its origins are rather more utilitarian. In the early days of printing, it was the quickest and most effective method of colouring black-and-white wood block engravings and transferring designs on to fabric. Stencilled lettering has long been a quick method for manufacturers to transfer information on to packaging. The Shaker community used tin sheets pierced with fine lettering to label the vegetable seeds harvested from their fields and, in the 19th century, Italian fruit growers from the Mediterranean port of Sorrento developed the stencilled labels on their lemon crates into a fine art. Even today, stencils are used to mark crates of whisky in Scottish distilleries and wooden boxes of salted pilchards in Penzance, at the far west tip of England.

Stencilled design has also been used for adding pattern to domestic pottery, especially in France and Eastern Europe. Hungarian and Czech bowls of the mid-20th century were embellished with spot or border designs of flower baskets, fruit, vines and animals, in rich folk-art style. These designs were transferred by painting a coloured slip glaze through a stamped tin stencil, specially shaped to fit within the biscuit-fired dish. Three or more stencils could be used to build up the most detailed patterns. As technology advanced, the airbrush replaced the stencil brush, giving a smoother surface to the colour. The trompe l'oeil plate project is a witty re-interpretation of these popular ceramics.

AMERICAN FOLK ART

Stencilled interiors reached their peak of popularity and expertise along the Eastern seaboard of the United States in the early 19th century. The elaborate wallpapers and woven carpets that settlers had enjoyed in Europe were no longer available, and home owners looked to paint as a way of creating decorative effects. Stencilling became a recognized trade and itinerant artists, such as J. Gleason of Rhode Island and Moses Eaton in New England, would travel from house to house, adding stencilled pineapples, garlands, swags and hearts to marbled and wood-grain effects.

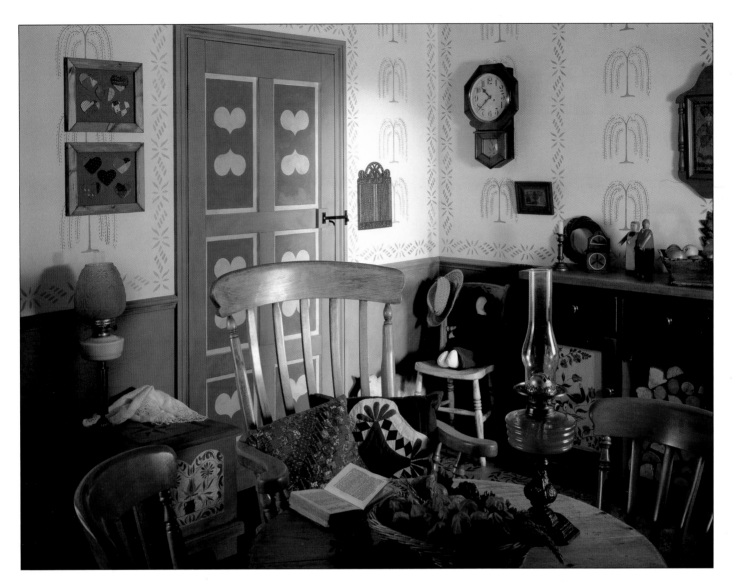

ABOVE: Stencilling allowed poorer people to copy styles found in grander homes and public buildings across Europe.

OPPOSITE: Floral motifs are always popular.

Colour schemes, as now, depended largely on the taste of individual clients and ranged from subtle grey walls with simple repeated patterns to sunshine yellow with red and green flowers. Nowadays we go to great lengths to ensure patterns match exactly and that all our repeats line up, but surviving folk art walls were painted with a great panache that reveals a careless disregard for accuracy, visible brush marks and the occasional smudge.

VICTORIAN GOTHIC

The Victorians used stencilling to add formal decoration to the interiors of public buildings such as churches, synagogues, stations, art galleries and town halls. Many of these original schemes have been refurbished to dazzling effect. As much surviving Victorian needlework and paintwork has faded over the decades, it is useful to remember just how bright the original threads and paints actually were. A recently discovered stencilling scheme of 1863 by Alexander Thomson (the leading Scottish architect of his day) shows a surprisingly bright range of colours: Pompeiian red, bottle green and gold leaf. He included an eclectic combination of neo-classical, Asian and Egyptian motifs on the murals and borders of Lilybank House in Glasgow. Restoration work on London's Midland Hotel, built at the height of the railway boom, has revealed complex multicoloured stencilling schemes that originally extended down long corridors and across vaulted ceilings. Most of these were painted over by succeeding generations, for whom such intense pattern proved difficult to live alongside.

ARTS AND CRAFTS

At the end of the 19th century, a new aesthetic movement transformed the decorative arts. Art nouveau, and the subsequent Arts and Crafts movement, was a fresh way of looking at natural subjects. Building on the inspiration of artists such as William Morris and the arts of Eastern cultures, the slavish realism and overblown ornamentation of the Victorian era was simplified into flowing, graceful forms. The stylized, two-dimensional patterns of this era were ideally suited to stencilling and with the growing enthusiasm for crafts, particularly among women, it became a highly popular method of decorating the home.

The advent of electric lighting meant that rooms were lighter and brighter than they had ever been, and the fussiness of the parlour

ABOVE: The organic forms and patterns of the art nouveau period make excellent stencil designs for tiles, walls and borders.

RIGHT: The repeated paisley pattern creates a wallpaper effect in this small study.

was gradually replaced by pale walls and uncluttered surfaces. The epitome of this new look was Charles Rennie Mackintosh's unique "Glasgow Style". Considered radical at the time, his elegant interiors are the precursor of late 20th century minimalism. He used stencilling as an unobtrusive way to add flat colour and pattern to canvas chair backs, bed hangings and upholstered seating. His favourite motifs of roses and sinuous plant forms have been much imitated and reproduced.

In America at the same time, larger scale stencils in a slightly softer style became highly popular. Continuous border designs encircled rooms, running both above and below plate and dado (chair) rails, and large friezes filled

the deep areas below picture rails. Single stencils, repeated motifs and overall patterns were all used, and stylized flora and fauna – birds, fish, insects and animals – were a favourite theme.

ART DECO

As the soft lines of art nouveau gave way to the more angular shapes of art deco, so stencilled patterns changed. *The Practical Guide to Stencilling* by Frank Gibson, published in 1926, featured an array of motifs and all-over designs including the characteristic sunray pattern. Other enduring stencil designs – many of which appear in modern form in this book – included were Greek key borders, twining vines and bunches of grapes, fleurs-de-lys,

ABOVE: Pale light blues and candy tones are popular contemporary colours.

ABOVE RIGHT: Focusing the attention on one wall is a modern use of stencils – use large single motifs, such as this branch of delicate orange blossom.

butterflies and (at the time when Tutankhamun's tomb was causing a sensation) an Egyptian scarab. The most intricate of all is a detailed reproduction of the willow pattern plate design in traditional blue and white.

Gibson's book suggests a wide range of textiles considered suitable for stencilling, which provide an interesting insight into the wide range of domestic linens to be found in an ordinary household. They include not just table cloths, but also runners, napkins and mats. Some of the decorated items are still to be found and many of them are still subjects for stencilling: lampshades, cushions, curtains and picture frames. Others – collar boxes, shaving paper holders, bookcase curtains and mantel borders – are now obsolete, but the idea of stencilling garden paling is charming and one that could be copied for a cottage-style plot.

SWEDISH STYLE

One of the most influential decorating styles of recent years derives from the Gustavian look of 19th-century Sweden. The short days and long winters of Scandinavian countries mean that people spend a lot of time indoors, and interior colour schemes are predominantly pale in tone: cream, light blue and sage green provide the backdrop for highlights of dusky pink, cherry red and the favourite blue.

Artist Carl Larsson's book *My Home* introduced this style to a wider audience, who relished the detailed paintings of his wife and children in a house decorated with simple furniture, striped and checked fabric, and restrained stencilling. Small florals, looped ribbon bows, hearts and wheatsheaves all echo the embroidery designs of the period and region and were used on walls, floors and furniture. Any stencilling done in this style should be done in pale colours and gently aged by rubbing it lightly with abrasive paper to give an authentic look.

CONTEMPORARY STENCILS

Interior design of the 1980s tended towards the flouncy and floral, and gave stencilling a reputation as fiddly and over-decorated. Since then, there has been a great turnaround in style. "New vintage" effects pay homage to the past, but are to be found in bright, clear shades with none of the fussiness of their original inspiration. Drawing on a wealth of historic decorative styles, new designers are reworking antique motifs such as oriental blossoms, paisleys and lace patterns in a bold, graphic manner, using new colours and shades.

The primary colours, flamboyant flowers and geometric patterns of 1970s wallpaper have already made a comeback, and they look more at home within the proportions of modern loft-style apartments and open living spaces than they ever did in suburban bedrooms and sitting rooms. These patterns are filtering through to stencil design, such as in the form of pop-art style canvases. By playing with scale – enlarging a single flower to cover a cushion – interior designers are creating a new, modern look.

STENCILLING BASICS

The appeal of stencilling as a decorative technique lies in its immediacy. Getting started is easy, as it requires only a few basic materials and items of equipment, and no special painting skills. Even a complete beginner can achieve stunning results in a short time. The following pages show you how to make a stencil and how to use it, and suggest ways in which you can produce your own individual interpretations of the designs in the book to suit your own style and interior decoration.

ABOVE: Making sketches and transferring your designs to stencil card or acetate can be very rewarding.

LEFT: Stencil brushes are available in many shapes and dimensions. It is important to clean them after every session to keep them in good condition.

STENCILLING EQUIPMENT

Making a stencil is a straightforward process that does not entail buying a huge amount of equipment. Some of the items you may already have around the house, and others are readily available from good art and craft suppliers. As with any other creative task, it is worth investing in the best tools for the job, in order to achieve a professional result. If you plan to make a lot of acetate stencils, for example, using a heat knife will save a great deal of time and a self-healing cutting mat is essential for safe stencil making.

MEASURING AND MARKING EQUIPMENT

Accurate measuring is important when planning the final position of a stencil. You may need to mark up a wall, box lid or greetings card with registration marks – and when drawing up the stencil itself. Set squares (triangles) give accurate corners and right angles and a metal ruler has a dual role, for measuring and as a straight edge to guide the knife when cutting straight lines within a stencil. Graph paper can be used for planning more formal designs and enlarging a template if you do not have access to a photocopier.

A retractable tape measure is essential for marking up a wall scheme or other large surface, but a dressmaker's measure will do for smaller areas. Light pencil marks and guidelines on wood, walls or paper can easily be removed with an eraser when the paint is dry. Water-soluble or fading fabric marking pens can be used to mark up fabric.

TRACING AND TRANSFERRING EQUIPMENT

Traditional orange or yellow stencil card is treated with linseed oil (which gives it its characteristic smell) to make it pliable, easy to cut and waterproof. Use a sheet of carbon paper or tracing paper (and a soft pencil) and a ballpoint pen to copy a design on to the card. If you are using clear or semi-transparent acetate, there is no need to transfer the design before cutting out. Adhesive stencil film

LEFT: Measuring and marking equipment: *1 metal ruler, 2 graph paper, 3 tape measure, 4 eraser, 5 fabric marking pen, 6 pencils, 7 set squares.*

RIGHT: Tracing and transferring equipment: 1 *adhesive stencil film, 2 stencil card, 3 acetate, 4 carbon paper, 5 tracing paper, 6 hard pencil, 7 soft pencil, 8 ballpoint pen.*

used for airbrushing and other graphic work is ideal for intricate one-off stencils on glass or ceramic surfaces. The design can simply be traced through it with a sharp hard pencil.

FIXING AND CUTTING EQUIPMENT

If you only intend to make one or two stencils you can cut them on to a piece of thick card (stock), but this tends to blunt any knife quite quickly. Alternatively, a durable self-healing cutting mat will prove invaluable, as it protects the blade and is much safer. If you need extra stability, fix your tracing paper or acetate on to the mat with low-tack masking tape, which will not damage either surface, and a coating of spray mount, which is a light adhesive that can easily be repositioned and does not leave any residue.

When cutting out, you should always work with a sharp blade, which will give a cleaner line and is easier to use. Choose a snap-off knife, which has a supply of new tips, or a craft knife into which new blades can be fitted. A heat knife melts quickly through plastic and speeds up the process: always place a sheet of glass over the design being traced.

RIGHT: Fixing and cutting equipment: 1 *self-healing cutting mat, 2 spray mount, 3 heat knife, 4 low-tack masking tape, 5 snap-off knife, 6 craft knife.*

BRUSHES AND PAINTS

There are various different methods of applying colour to a stencil and many different types of paint that can be used. Small pots of creamy oil-based colour and oil crayons are specially made for use with stencils, but water-based acrylics are easy to use and can be bought from any good art or craft supplier. Special stencil brushes are, however, an essential purchase and the initial outlay of buying a range of several different sizes will prove worthwhile. With care, they will last you for years.

BRUSHES

Stencil brushes are short-handled and their round flat heads are densely packed with firm bristles to let you control the flow of paint. Sizes range from about 5mm to 4cm/¼in to 1½in. Smaller brushes are intended for detailed areas and big ones will cover large areas very quickly. Some have short, stiff bristles for stippling and others are slightly longer and more flexible for a softer, swirled effect. It is worth investing in a good set of stencil brushes. Do not let your brushes or sponges dry out or they will be ruined. It is important to keep your equipment in good condition.

Decorator's brushes are for painting in backgrounds and colour washes. Choose a size to suit your needs. Artist's brushes are used for adding fine details. A sponge roller is another quick way to apply flat colour, while a natural sea sponge, which is better than an artificial one, will produce interesting textures.

RIGHT: Brushes and paints: *1 Stencil brushes in different sizes, 2 decorator's brushes, 3 fine artist's brushes, 4 sponge roller, 5 natural sea sponge, 6 artist's acrylic paint, 7 emulsion (latex) paints, 8 spray paint, 9 fabric medium, 10 paint tray, 11 emulsion (latex) paint swatches.*

PAINTS

Emulsion (latex) paint is used for painting plastered or paper-covered walls. Sample pots (in the same colour range as the room scheme) are a good source of historic and unusual colours for stencilling. Artist's acrylic paint comes in tubes and acrylic craft paint in pots. The latter is very versatile and can be mixed with fabric medium for use on textiles or texture gels to give a variety of three-dimensional effects. Glass and ceramic paints can be used for stencilling, but have to be baked in a hot oven to fix the colour.

Spray paint is fast and easy, and any aerosol from car colour to granite-effect craft spray can be used for stencils. A paint tray or ceramic palette will keep colours separate and is useful for mixing shades with a brush, but a saucer or tile serves the same purpose and is more useful for sponging.

HOW TO MAKE A STENCIL

A stencil is a negative image of a finished design. The basic shapes that form the image are cut from stencil card or acetate and the links that are left between the spaces are called "ties".

CARD STENCILS

Stencil card – lightly oiled Manila board – is strong and durable. It is particularly useful if you are going to repeat a design many times. Plastic stencil film is less long-lasting but quicker to use and easy to cut.

It also saves time when working on multi-layered or continuous designs. Using a heat knife (a pointed tool, which melts through the plastic) will speed up the stencil-making process even further.

Using tracing paper

When transferring a design with tracing paper use this method for an actual-size template. Fix tracing paper over the design with low-tack masking tape, then draw over the outlines using a sharp pencil. Remove the tape and turn the paper over. Rub the back of the lines with a soft pencil. Turn the paper and tape it centrally to a piece of stencil card, then redraw the shapes with a ballpoint pen.

Using carbon paper

When transferring a design with carbon paper, enlarge or reduce the template to the required size on a scanner or a photocopier. Place the copy centrally on the stencil board and slip a piece of carbon paper, face down, underneath. Tape the edges securely to the stencil board with low-tack masking tape. Draw carefully around each outline with a ballpoint pen, pressing firmly but smoothly.

Cutting out

Tape the stencil card securely to a self-healing cutting mat or a piece of thick card (stock) with low-tack masking tape. Using a sharp-bladed craft knife, cut along each line at a time within the shapes. It is much easier to start with the largest elements of the stencil, then tackle the more detailed, intricate areas. Always cut towards yourself turning the board with your free hand as necessary, but with care, to create smooth curves. Don't worry if you slice through a tie (one of the card "bridges" that link the cut out shapes): they are easily repaired with adhesive tape.

PLASTIC STENCILS

The benefit of using plastic stencils such as acetate is that you do not have to transfer the design but can cut the shape out directly.

Preparing to cut

Place a sheet of glass (tape the edges if they are rough) over the page of the book or photocopy you have chosen. Cut a piece of plastic at least 5cm/2in larger all round than the design and tape it to the glass with low-tack masking tape. Peel this off carefully when the stencil is complete. For extra security, you can lightly spray the back with spray mount.

Using a craft knife

Always use a sharp craft knife to cut around each element within the design as for a card stencil, but take extra care because the blade is more liable to slip on the smooth surface of the glass than it is on card. Remove the tape, lift the design and check that nothing has been missed out. Neaten any rough edges with the knife or a small pair of curved blade scissors.

Using a heat knife

When cutting out with a knife, read the manufacturer's instructions carefully before starting and practise on an offcut or spare piece of acetate to get the hang of using the knife before you start. Always use a sharp blade to give a cleaner line and make sure the blade is secure. Trace the point of the knife steadily around each outline, without pressing too hard and keeping an even pressure. If you work too slowly the line will be too wide so trace each element smoothly in a single motion.

APPLYING COLOUR

There are several different ways of colouring in a stencil with acrylic paints, using a brush, sponge or foam roller, each of which produces its own individual look. Take inspiration from the suggestions shown here, then go on to create your own special effects to suit your own ideas.

BRUSH EFFECTS

A single stencil can be used in many ways by applying paint in different colours and textures. The examples on the next few pages show you how to create just some of the many possible paint effects. Experiment and try them out before you start work on an actual project. Start off by securing the stencil to the surface being decorated with masking tape (use the low-tack version which will not damage the background) or spray mount. This adhesive keeps the whole stencil flat, reducing the risk of paint seeping under the edges, but should only be used in a well-ventilated space. Wipe the stencil clean of paint and glue when you have finished working. An acetate stencil can be washed in soapy water and dried on kitchen paper.

Using a stencil brush

Dip the flat tip of the stencil brush into a saucer of paint, then remove the surplus by rubbing the bristles on to kitchen paper in a circular motion. Avoid overloading: it is better to apply two light coats of paint rather than one heavy one. Always wash the bristles in warm soapy water when the paint builds up and when changing colours – a quick blast from a hairdryer will speed up the drying process.

Blocked colour

Always hold the brush lightly at right angles when stencilling, so that the paint will not get underneath the stencil itself and smudge the outline. Load the brush and dab it up and down within the stencil. You should be making a tapping movement rather than sweeping the brush as when painting. Build up the paint gradually to produce a solid block of colour and wait until it is dry before removing the stencil.

Stippled colour

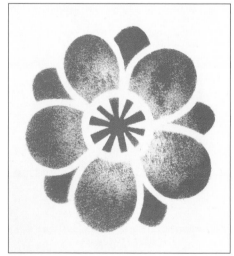

This technique can be used to create differently shaded elements within a stencil to give the finished design an almost three-dimensional appearance. Block the colour as above for the darkest parts (around the outer edge of the petals in this example) and apply the same colour much more sparsely to the lighter areas. Take time to build up layers of colour and rework the stencil until you are pleased with the result.

Using more than one colour

If you are using two or more colours on a stencil, it is important to use just one paint at a time, changing or washing the brushes in between use to keep the elements distinct and the colours clean. If the different coloured sections are adjacent, use strips of low-tack masking tape or a piece of paper to protect the areas that are not being painted.

Multicoloured stippling

It is possible to create a huge range of textures and great depth of colour by applying several colours to a stencil. Here the outside edges of the petals have been stippled in solid pink, which fades through to a soft orange. In contrast, the star-shaped flower centre is more solid and the dense colour of the leaves is broken up with pink stippling.

Dry brushing

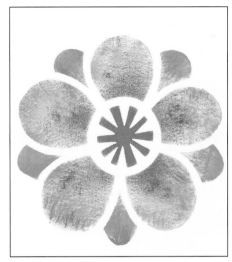

As its name suggests, this paint effect uses only a very small amount of paint. Load the stencil brush, then wipe most of the paint off on to kitchen paper. Fill in the shapes with light, straight strokes, allowing a little of the background colour to show through as you apply each successive layer. Here, all the strokes have been made from the centre outwards.

Using a sponge

Sponging is a good way to fill a large or small stencil with interesting texture. You can use a synthetic household sponge for dense colour, but natural sponges give a more open and varied effect. Dip the sponge into the paint, remove the excess by dabbing it on to newspaper or kitchen towel then dab it lightly over the stencil.

Using a roller

Sponge rollers can be used to apply a coat of a single colour or, as here, to produce subtly blended effects. Put a blob of each paint in a saucer, in a short line. Push the dry roller over the paint and roll it backwards and forwards until the edges are blurred, then roll it over the stencil.

Stippling from the edges

Using a very dry stencil brush (dab most of the paint off the bristles before you start), stipple from the outside of the design, working inwards. By the time you get to the centre, there should be hardly any paint left on your brush, ensuring a very soft paint effect in this area.

PAINT EFFECTS

A stencil brush, versatile as it may be, is not the only way to apply paint through a stencil. Sponging and rolling are both very quick and effective alternative techniques, particularly if you are going to repeat the design across a large area, such as a wall. As with brush effects, it is a good idea to have several sponges or brushes to hand when working on a stencil that uses more than one colour. Pour a small amount of each paint into a separate saucer so that the colours do not become mixed.

Sponge effect

The open texture of a natural sponge makes it ideal for building up layers of colour. The holes within it produce round or oval spaces within the paint surface, which means that the previous layers are still visible. Try not to cover the background completely as a few white speckles make the finished design look bright and lively.

Sponge roller effect

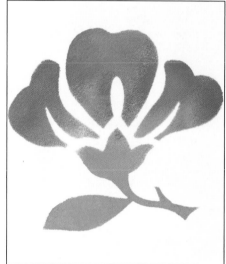

Sponge rollers – cylinders of sponge fixed on to a plastic handle – come in widths from 2.5cm/1in up to 15cm/6in. Use narrow ones for details and wider ones for applying a first coat to the stencil or covering bigger spaces. When working on a multicoloured design, mask off the areas that are not to be painted, because the roller is not as precise as a brush.

Adding a drop shadow

A drop shadow is a deceptively simple way of giving a sophisticated feeling of depth to a flat motif. Decide where the finished design is to go, then position the stencil slightly below and to the right of that position. Stipple the right-hand side of the design lightly in grey paint. When dry, stencil the main design above and to the left of the shadow.

Adding texture

There are several different texture gels available from good craft stores, all designed for use with artist's acrylic paints. The gels range from ground pumice stone to very small plastic balls, or metallic glitter. They are stirred into the paint, which is then stippled thickly on to the stencil. A simple do-it-yourself grainy texture can, however, easily be produced by adding grains of sand to acrylic paint or using powdered multipurpose filler.

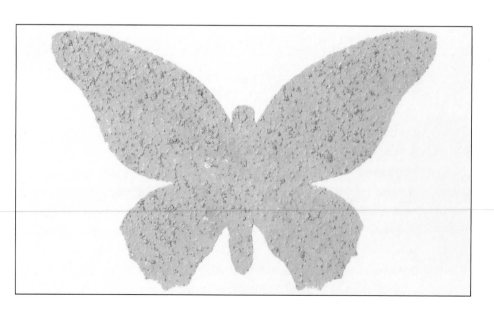

SPECIAL PAINTS

Several of the projects in this book use artist's acrylic paint, which has many advantages. It is relatively cheap and economic to use, readily available, and it comes in a wide spectrum of colours and can be mixed to create myriad others. It also dries quickly and can be washed from brushes, rollers or sponges with warm, soapy water. There are, of course, many alternatives, each of which has its own individual character and purpose. Some of them are illustrated here and once you have tried them, search the shelves of your local art store and experiment with glitter paints, wax crayons, oil sticks, translucent glass paints or watercolours.

Using spray paint

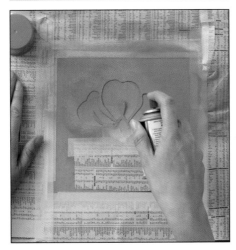

When using an aerosol it is important that you mask off the surrounding area completely with sheets of newspaper. However carefully you spray the paint, small particles inevitably hover in the air and will mark any background that has not been covered. You should also work in a well-ventilated room or outdoors.

Spray paint effects

Mask off with card or masking tape all the parts of the stencil that are not being used before applying the first colour. Press the button and move the can across the surface a few times. Build up several thin layers of paint, rather than one thick one, which will form a pool and seep under the edges of the stencil.

Fabric paint

Wash and press the fabric or garment before stencilling to remove any residue from the manufacturing process. Tape a length of spare fabric on to a pad of newspaper (to absorb any excess paint that goes through the fabric), or insert a piece of card (stock) inside a garment to protect the back. Once it is dry, heat-fix the paint according to the manufacturer's instructions.

Ceramic paint

Adhesive stencil film, used by graphic artists, is very useful when painting on glass or ceramic surfaces. Trace the design in pencil, then remove the backing and stick the film to a clean surface. Use a sharp craft knife to cut out the shapes, and apply the paint sparingly with a brush, sponge or roller. The finished object should then be fired by baking it in the oven, as instructed by the manufacturer.

Metallic wax

This creamy wax, used by gilders and picture framers, comes in a range of metallic shades from pale platinum and gold through to bronze and pewter. Apply it by wrapping your forefinger in a piece of soft cloth and rubbing your fingertip over the surface of the wax. Transfer it to the stencil by rubbing in small circles until the surface appears burnished. More than one colour can be applied for a luxurious effect: apply the lightest shade first.

REGISTRATION MARKS

If a stencil has more than one component, the two parts must line up exactly. This is easy with acetate stencils, as the first layer of paint will be visible. It is more difficult with card stencils, so registration marks – small crosses or notches – cut into both stencils in the same position are used. They are transferred by pencil and the overlay is positioned so that the lines show through the second set of registration marks. Use them also for a repeated border where the motifs overlap to create the finished design.

BORDERS AND TWO-LAYERED STENCILS

Elegant stencilled borders provide the finishing touch in a room. They are ideal for creating "frames" and panel effects. Use them to define space, such as a dado (chair) rail or to create a painted border around a floor.

Using a card stencil for a border

Each repeated motif should be positioned at the same level. Once you have transferred the stencil on to card, draw a line along the bottom edge of the design, continuing it out to the left and right edges. Draw a line and match the two up for each repeat. Transfer the registration marks at the beginning and end of each repeat on to the card and cut notches at these points. Transfer the second notch on to the surface with a pencil "V" and match the first notch up to this point each time the stencil is used.

Using acetate for a border

Clear sheets of acetate are much easier to use than card when stencilling borders. You can line them up by eye, rather than by using registration marks. It is still, however, important to draw a baseline on to the surface so that the stencil will be straight and horizontal. For two-layered stencils, the design can be lined up by eye. You can also transfer the registration marks with a waterproof pen and make small slits along them. Pencil a cross within these marks when the first layer has been finished and match the second stencil to them.

Two-layered stencils

When transferring the two elements that make up the design on to stencil card, draw in the cross-shaped registration marks. Carefully cut out each stencil, then rule in pencil lines to join up the four crosses, making a rectangle or square. Snip out the corners to make right-angled notches. Before removing the first stencil, make a two-sided pencil mark like an arrow tip along each corner. Position the second stencil within these marks and it will then be aligned precisely to the first.

ONE-OFF AND REVERSE STENCILS

Stencil-making does not always have to be time-consuming and formal, nor does it require specialist equipment. These one-off techniques show that stencilled decoration can also be spontaneous and unstructured. Use them for stationery or paper projects such as greetings cards or wrapping paper, or let your imagination run wild and stencil lacy patterns on to a silk scarf or a flurry of leaf outlines across a wall. Instead of starting with a negative image, as with a regular stencil, reverse stencils are in fact positive images, with outlines defined by the paint. Found natural objects, such as ferns or dried, pressed leaves, are a good source of unexpected shapes, or try using lace or paper doilies.

Using leaves

Collect a selection of interestingly shaped autumn leaves and press them under a heavy book overnight. To use them as stencils, hold the leaf down with the fingers of one hand or fix to the surface with a reusable putty adhesive and block in colour around the edge, using a wide brush loaded with paint.

Using lace

Use a brush or aerosol spray paint to transfer the intricate designs of woven lace without distorting the fabric. Fix the lace on to the surface to be decorated with spray mount and mask off the surrounding area. Spray two or more light coats of paint across the surface, using even strokes, until the pattern is well defined.

Paper cuts

Simple, symmetrical designs that are going to be used just once can be cut from thin coloured paper. Fold the paper in half vertically and draw one side of a heart along the crease with a pencil. Cut out the shape with sharp scissors and flatten out the paper, then stencil as usual. Once you have mastered this quick and versatile technique, you could go on to make more complex designs, such as paper snowflakes, Christmas trees, or chains of little figures.

VARIATIONS ON A THEME

The stencils that appear in this book have each been designed with a specific project in mind – a complex wall treatment, a kitchen curtain, a cushion or a simple greetings card. All of them, however, can be altered and reinterpreted endlessly. There are many ways in which you can vary colour schemes, invert or reverse the motif, change the spacing, enlarge or reduce the design, or print it on an unexpected surface. Here are some ideas for creating different layouts and patterns. Use a little imagination, and you will be able to come up with countless variations of your own.

Positive and negative images

The negative image on the left – a pale flower branch in a single colour on a very dark green background – is a graphic design. It is, in fact, exactly the same design as the delicate spray on the right – a positive image that has been stencilled more conventionally in colour on white paper. Light-on-dark images always have strong visual impact. Try stencilling a white pattern on a pastel background for a more subtle, but still unusual look.

Mirror image

Any stencil design that is not symmetrical can be flipped over to create its mirror image. Paint the first motif as usual. Clean off any surplus paint from the stencil and leave it to dry. Turn it over, line up the stencil carefully opposite the first motif, and block in the second motif. This is a good way to create a simple border, by stencilling pairs of reversed motifs above a dado (chair) rail or below a ceiling coving (cove molding).

Repeating around a point

This pattern, in which a roughly square design has been repeated four times around a centre point, is reminiscent of a tiled wall. It can be copied with any symmetrical stencil. Draw two lines that intersect at right angles, then two more at 45 degrees to the first pair. Mark the base of the first motif, close to the centre point, then line the stencil up along the diagonal line. Stencil three more motifs on the diagonals, ensuring that they all start at the same distance along the lines.

Random repeats

A small, self-contained motif like this butterfly or a floral motif can be repeated at random across the surface. Use a single colour, or stencil each one in a different shade to produce a lively, interesting pattern, which would work equally well on a wall or on fabric.

Changing sizes

This pattern uses a pretty Japanese flower, which has been enlarged to make a bigger stencil. The combination of the two sizes gives vitality to the design, and shows just how many different ways there are of using a very simple motif to produce a sophisticated result.

Rotating with blocked leaves

Using a very dry brush with a tiny amount of paint, rotate the bristles in a circular motion. This rotating action leaves enough paint on the surface for a lighter, softer look than a block application. Use the same effect in a darker colour on the inside of the petals.

Rotating and soft shading

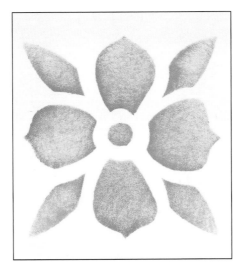

Using a very dry brush with a tiny amount of paint, place your brush on one side of the stencil and rotate the brush in small circles. Repeat this action, using a slightly darker colour on the edges of the stencil, to create the effect of soft shading.

Rotating and shading in two colours

This is a similar effect to rotating and soft shading, but is more directional. Using a very dry brush with a tiny amount of paint, place your brush in the centre of the flower and rotate the bristles slightly outwards. Repeat this action, using a slightly darker colour.

HALF-DROP REPEATS

A regular repeated design looks very effective on a large expanse of wall, giving the illusion of a printed wallpaper pattern. Stencil a few motifs roughly on to sheets of paper, cut them out and tape them to the wall before you begin, to get an idea of the finished look.

The framework for the pattern should be measured up very carefully, especially in older houses where walls and windows may not be perfectly straight. Start by marking a vertical line down the left edge of the wall using chalked builder's string and bear in mind any fixed architectural features such as light fittings, chimney breasts (fireplace projections), architraves (trims), alcoves and corners that you will need to work around.

1 To mark up the wall, decide how far apart the motifs are to lie, horizontally and vertically. Cut a rectangle of card (stock) to these measurements and draw two lines to divide it into quarters. Cut a notch at each end of the lines. Use the card as a guide to draw a light pencil grid across the wall.

2 To stencil a half-drop repeat: in the same way, draw two lines across the stencil and notch the ends. Use these marks to match the stencil to the grid. Stencil in the first horizontal row of motifs, then position the next row in the spaces below. Continue until the wall is covered.

3 To make half-drop repeats on fabric, mark a grid on to fabric, decide how far apart the motifs are to be, then fold and press lightly along these lines. When the fabric is opened out these lines will appear as creases, which will disappear when the fabric is pressed once again.

PREPARING AND FINISHING

As with any home decorating project, whether it is painting an old wooden chair or putting a new paint effect on a wall, time invested in preparation pays off by giving you a professional result at the end. Don't be in too much of a hurry to start, plan carefully and work in an orderly way. Collect together all the equipment and tools you will need, including the cleaning materials for tidying up afterwards and a stack of old newspaper to protect the floor or work surface. An overall or smock will protect your clothes.

PREPARING WALLS

If you are working on a freshly plastered wall, make sure that it is completely dry before painting it with emulsion (latex) paint in your desired base colour. However clean they appear, previously decorated surfaces should always be washed down well with detergent or sugar soap to remove accumulated dust and grease. If you wish your stencils to have a more textured background than that which is given by flat emulsion paint, try using one of these simple paint effects on the wall.

Most modern acrylic paints are tough and waterproof, but your finished stencils may need to be sealed, especially in humid areas such as kitchens and bathrooms, or if they are in rooms which receive lots of wear and tear such as hallways and landings. Leave the painted surface to dry thoroughly for a week, then seal with matt (flat) varnish.

PREPARING WOOD

New or unprimed wood should be sanded down with medium- and then fine-grade abrasive paper. When the surface is smooth, wipe it over with a damp cloth to remove any residual dust and leave to dry. If you wish to darken the natural colour, use a wood stain, diluting it with water for a lighter shade and painting it in long strokes along the grain. Otherwise, prepare with a clear wood sealer. Water-based sealants are easier to use and do not have the yellowish hue of their oil-based equivalents. When the stencilling is complete, apply two coats of water-based varnish to give a hardwearing finish to the wood.

Colour washing

This can be done with a light paint on a darker background or vice versa, or for a more subtle look with two very closely toning colours. Dilute the second coat with water, adding more water for a lighter colour, then paint it on the wall using loose brushstrokes painted in one or many directions, or use a wide roller.

Sponging

Using a natural sea sponge creates an open texture and is a quick way to cover a large surface. Wash and rinse the sponge, then squeeze out the excess moisture. Dip it into a saucer of diluted emulsion (latex) paint then dab it on to the wall in a circular pattern or straight lines, depending on the effect required.

ABOVE: Always sand new or unprimed wood before stencilling to create a key.

WALLS AND SURFACES

Whether you wish to recreate an American folk art interior, paint an Indian-inspired Paisley design to imitate wallpaper or add a bold one-off mural to your living space, a plain-coloured wall provides the perfect backdrop for large-scale stencilled design. This chapter also includes borders for walls and floors, a clever trompe l'oeil row of plates and ideas for enhancing architectural features such as fireplaces and windows.

ABOVE: These pretty faux plates add interest behind a plain country kitchen shelf.

LEFT: A repeated border adds style and individuality to simple white-washed floorboards.

GREEK URNS

Classic Greek urns softly outlined under a warm terracotta colourwash have a very Mediterranean feel. The stencilling is worked in clear varnish so that the top colour slides over without adhering, leaving very subtly coloured motifs. Arrange the urns randomly over the wall for an informal and rustic finish. This effect works well in a kitchen or dining room and on slightly uneven walls. You can try different colour combinations or use a slightly stronger coloured emulsion (latex) paint to create a bolder look. Other classic motifs include scrolls, abstract geometric shapes, animals, marine life, fruits, flora and fauna.

You will need

- emulsion (latex) paints in cream and terracotta
- large household sponge
- acetate sheet
- craft knife and self-healing cutting mat
- masking tape
- stencil brush
- satin acrylic varnish
- wallpaper paste
- clean cotton rag

1 Working in rough, sweeping strokes, rub a base coat of cream emulsion (latex) paint over the wall using a sponge. Trace the urn template at the back of the book and cut a stencil from acetate sheet using a sharp-bladed craft knife and cutting mat. Tape it to the wall and stencil with varnish. Reposition the stencil and cover the wall with randomly arranged urns.

2 Make up the wallpaper paste following the manufacturer's instructions on the pack. Mix one part terracotta emulsion with one part paste. This will make the colourwash slimy and slow down the drying time, preventing "joins" in the finished colourwash. Using a clean household sponge, dab lumps of the mixture over about 1m/3¼ft square of the wall.

3 Immediately rub the wall in a clockwise circular motion to blur the sponge marks.

4 Continue dabbing on paint and blurring with the sponge to cover the whole wall. The varnished urns should be revealed underneath the colourwash.

5 If the urns are not clear enough, use a slightly damp rag and your index finger to rub off a little more colourwash from the varnished shapes. This can be done even after the wall has dried.

ABOVE: Experiment with other colour combinations. Try colourwashing duck-egg blue emulsion (latex) paint over a beige emulsion background as an alternative.

RIGHT: The stencils are placed at random and the effect is very subtle.

TROMPE-L'OEIL PLATES

A shelf full of decorative painted plates adds a witty touch to a kitchen corner. Follow these plate designs or translate your own patterned china into stencils to give a co-ordinated look. Why not add some individual plates to the wall as well?

1 Cut three pieces of stencil card 30cm/12in square. Mark the centre of each card by measuring the centre of each edge and ruling a horizontal and a vertical line across each card to join the marks.

2 Draw a line 3.5cm/1¼in in from all four edges of each card. Place the plate in the centre of the card and draw around the edge. Cut out the plate shape from the first piece of stencil card (stencil 1).

3 Using a pair of compasses, draw a circle from the centre point about 4cm/1½in from the edge of the plate on the two remaining pieces of yellow stencil card.

4 Trace or photocopy the plate template at the back of the book to the desired size and carefully transfer the floral design to the second piece of stencil card.

5 Cut out the design using a craft knife and cutting mat. Cut out the smaller areas first and the larger areas last (stencil 2). On the third piece of stencil card, cut out the inner circle (stencil 3).

6 Draw a faint horizontal pencil line on the wall and put two marks 30cm/12in apart on the line to act as a guide for positioning the stencils. Spray the back of the plate stencil (1) with spray mount and place in position on the wall. Press down firmly to ensure a good contact. Mask off the surrounding area with paper and masking tape, leaving no gaps. Wearing a protective face mask, spray white and cream spray paint on to the stencil. Remove the masks and stencil.

7 Attach the flower stencil (2) to the wall with spray mount, lining it up with the marks on the wall. Mask off the surrounding area. Stick small pieces of masking tape over the leaves on the stencil. Wearing a protective face mask, spray the flowers with pinks and mauves, applying a fine layer of paint in short sharp puffs. Try each paint colour on the mask surrounding the stencil to test the colour and to make sure that the nozzle is clear.

8 Remove the masking tape from the leaves. Fold a small piece of stencil card in half and use it to shield the rest of the stencil from any spray paint. Spray the leaves using light and dark green paints, trying not to get too much green on the flowers.

▶

9 Cut a small hole in a piece of stencil card and use it to spray the centres of the flowers green.

10 Hold the shield of card around the dot designs on the border, and spray each one with red paint. Spray blue paint over the wavy lines on the border. Again, do not apply too much paint. Remove the masks then carefully remove the stencil.

11 Spray the back of the last stencil (3) with spray mount and position it on the wall. Mask off the surrounding area as before. Spray a fine mist of grey paint over the top left-hand side and bottom right-hand side of the plate design to create a shadow. Aim the nozzle slightly away from the stencil to ensure that hardly any paint hits the wall. Remove the masks and stencil.

12 Reposition stencil 1 on the wall and spray a very fine mist of blue paint around the edge of the plate. Repeat all stages along the edge of the shelf length.

RIGHT: The design for these trompe l'oeil plates can be adapted to the colour scheme in your kitchen or to match your own crockery.

KITCHEN ALCOVE

Stencil rows of china crockery and glassware along shelves to create a trompe l'oeil effect. This stencil would also make a great backdrop to a set of real shelves in a kitchen alcove. You can use emulsion (latex) paints to suit your own kitchen colour scheme or follow the colourways given here.

You will need

- masking tape
- spirit level
- tracing paper and pen
- acetate or stencil card
- craft knife and self-healing cutting mat
- soft pencil
- ceramic tile
- flat paintbrush
- stencil brush
- emulsion (latex) paints in dark sage green and cream
- eraser

1 Stick a length of masking tape across the wall to designate the top shelf. Check the level with a spirit level and adjust if necessary.

2 Stick a length of masking tape immediately above and below the first tape. Peel off the first tape. Mask the position of two more shelves 18cm/7in apart below the top shelf. Check the position of the shelves with a spirit level as before. Tape vertically across the ends of the shelves.

3 Trace the glassware and crockery templates at the back of the book. Cut out using a craft knife and cutting mat. You will need two stencils for each item – the glassware or crockery then the highlights.

4 Apply a thin coat of dark sage green paint on a ceramic tile with a flat paintbrush. Dab at the paint with a stencil brush and stencil the shelves holding the stencil brush upright and moving it in a circular motion.

5 Leave the paint to dry completely then carefully pull off the low-tack masking tape to reveal the straight edges of the shelves. You are now ready to stencil the glassware and the crockery.

6 Tape the bottle stencil to the wall, placing the lower registration marks on the lower edge of the top shelf. Mark the top registration marks and the top of the lower registration marks on the tape with a soft pencil. Stencil in the bottle.

7 Remove the stencil when it is completely dry. Tape the bottle highlight stencil to the wall, matching up the registration marks. Stencil the highlight in cream paint. Remove the stencil.

8 Tape the glass stencil to the wall, matching the lower right-hand registration mark of the bottle with the lower left-hand registration mark of the glass. Stencil the glass in dark sage green. Remove the stencil then stencil the highlight in cream.

9 Move the glass stencil along the wall, taping it in place matching the right-hand registration marks of the first glass with the left-hand registration marks of the second glass. Stencil the second glass and highlight as before. Continue stencilling a row of three glasses along the shelf always matching the registration marks.

10 Tape the cup stencil to the wall above the middle shelf, marking the registration marks as before. Stencil the cup in dark sage green then the highlight in cream. Move the stencil along the wall to work a row of three cups, matching the right-hand registration marks of the last cup with the left-hand registration marks of the next cup.

11 Tape the pot stencil to the wall above the bottom shelf, marking the registration marks as before. Stencil the pot in dark sage green. Leave to dry then remove the stencil. Tape the pot highlight stencil to the wall matching the registration marks. Stencil the highlights in cream paint. Remove the stencil.

12 Move along the bottom shelf to tape the bowls stencil to the wall above the bottom shelf, matching the lower right-hand registration mark of the pot with the lower left-hand registration mark of the bowls. Stencil the bowls in dark sage green then the highlights in cream. Erase the registration marks when complete.

FRENCH COUNTRY KITCHEN

This curtain design is adapted from the pattern on a French Art Deco soup bowl found in a fleamarket in Brussels. The flower design is also echoed in the hand-stencilled tiles and teams perfectly with the simple chequerboard border for a country look.

You will need

For the curtain:
- white muslin (cheesecloth) (see Measuring)
- iron
- newspaper
- masking tape
- stencil card
- craft knife and self-healing cutting mat
- spray mount
- blue stencil paint
- stencil brush
- pressing cloth
- needle
- white sewing thread
- tape measure
- dressmaker's chalk
- white cotton tape
- small pearl buttons

For the tiles:
- 10cm/4in square white tiles
- red spray paint

Measuring

To calculate the amount of muslin, allow:
1.5 x the width of the window plus
2.5cm/1in for each side hem, and add
7.5cm/3in to the length for hems.

1 Press the muslin (cheesecloth) to remove any creases, then fold it lengthways in accordion-style folds. Press lightly to mark the creases, then fold it widthways in accordion-style folds and press again. These squares will act as a guide for positioning the motifs. Cover the work surface with newspaper and tape down the muslin so that it is taut.

2 Trace the three floral templates and the border template at the back of the book and cut out the stencils from stencil card using a craft knife and cutting mat. Spray the back of one stencil with spray mount and, starting at the top right, lightly stencil the first motif.

3 Alternating the stencils as you work, stencil flowers in every other square over the whole curtain, leaving 15cm/6in free at the lower edge.

4 Stencil the blue chequerboard border along the bottom, lining up the stencil each time by matching the last two squares of the previous motif with the first two of the next stencil. Press the fabric well using a pressing cloth and iron.

5 Press under and slip-stitch a 1cm/½in double hem around the sides and lower edge of the curtains. Make a 2.5cm/1in double hem along the top edge.

6 Measure the top edge of the curtain and, using dressmaker's chalk, mark it into sections about 20cm/8in apart. Cut a 25cm/10in piece of cotton tape for each mark. Fold the first piece of tape in half and stitch to the back of the first mark. Sew a button on to the front of the curtain to anchor the tape. Repeat all the way along the edge then tie the finished curtain on to the curtain pole in bows.

7 For the tiles, cut a piece of stencil card to fit the tile. Cut out the three floral stencils using a craft knife and cutting mat.

8 Cover the work surface with newspaper. Using red spray paint, spray over the stencil lightly and evenly. Leave to dry, then remove the stencil.

RIGHT: *The co-ordinating tiles can be used individually as pot stands or set in the wall among plain white tiles.*

HERALDIC DINING ROOM

Lend an atmosphere of medieval luxury to your dining room with richly coloured walls and heraldic motifs stencilled in the same deep tones. Gilt accessories, heavy fabrics, brocades and a profusion of candles team well with this decor. All that remains is to prepare a sumptuous banquet.

You will need

- large household or decorator's sponges
- emulsion (latex) paints in camel, deep red and deep purple
- ruler
- spirit level
- pencil
- masking tape
- tracing paper
- acetate sheet
- craft knife and self-healing cutting mat
- stencil brushes
- fine lining brush

1 Using a large household or decorator's sponge, rub camel emulsion (latex) paint all over the wall. Leave to dry.

2 Repeat the process using a generous amount of deep red emulsion so that it almost covers the camel, giving a slightly mottled effect. Leave to dry.

ABOVE: Richly coloured walls and heraldic motifs are stencilled in the same deep tones to lend an atmosphere of luxury.

3 Using a ruler and spirit level, draw a light pencil line at dado (chair) rail height. Stick a line of low-tack masking tape just above it.

4 Sponge deep purple emulsion all over the wall below the masking tape to give a slightly mottled effect. Leave to dry completely, then remove the masking tape.

5 Trace the heraldic templates at the back of the book and cut the stencils from acetate sheet using a sharp-bladed craft knife and cutting mat. Secure the rose stencil above the dividing line and stencil in purple emulsion, using a stencil brush. When it is dry, position the fleur-de-lys stencil next to the rose and stencil in camel emulsion. Continue to alternate the stencils around the room.

6 Place the highlighting stencils over the painted motifs and, using a stencil brush, add purple highlights to the camel fleurs-de-lys and camel highlights to the purple roses.

7 Flip the stencils over and position as mirror images below the previously stencilled motifs. Stencil the roses in camel and the fleurs-de-lys in red.

8 Add in the highlights as before, using camel emulsion on the fleurs-de-lys and purple emulsion on the camel roses.

9 Using a fine lining brush and camel paint, paint a narrow line where the red and purple paints meet. If you do not have the confidence to do this freehand, position two rows of masking tape on the wall, leaving a small gap in between. When the line is dry, remove the tape.

OPPOSITE: Create a medieval dining room with these decorative stencils and add gilt accessories, heavy fabrics and a profusion of candles to complete the look.

CLASSICAL URN PANELS

A traditional Wedgwood blue colour scheme is ideal for this design of elegant urns set within a coach line frame. For a simpler effect, stencil the frame and omit the urns.

You will need

◆ low-tack masking tape
◆ scissors
◆ flat paintbrush
◆ emulsion (latex) paints in mid-blue and pale blue
◆ ceramic tile
◆ stencil brush
◆ piece of card (stock)
◆ tracing paper and pen
◆ stencil card
◆ craft knife and self-healing cutting mat
◆ metal ruler
◆ spray mount
◆ soft pencil

1 Using masking tape, mask off a rectangle at least 45cm/18in wide. Mask off another rectangle 1.5cm/⅝in inside the first rectangle to create a frame for the urn to sit within.

2 Cut four pieces of masking tape 6mm/¼in wide. Stick the tapes diagonally across the corners of the frame. This will create a three-dimensional effect when stencilled.

3 Using a flat paintbrush, spread a thin coat of mid-blue paint on to a ceramic tile. Dab at the paint with a stencil brush and stencil two adjacent sides of the frame. Protect the diagonal ends of the unpainted sides with a piece of card (stock).

▶

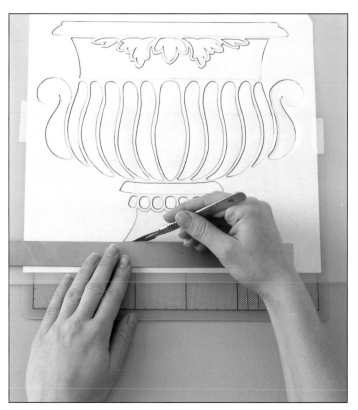

4 Blend the mid-blue and pale blue paint together and stencil the other sides of the frame. Leave to dry completely then peel off the tapes to reveal the neat, straight edges of the frame.

5 Trace the templates at the back of the book. Tape a piece of stencil card to the tracing. Using a craft knife and cutting mat cut out the stencils, cutting straight lines against a metal ruler.

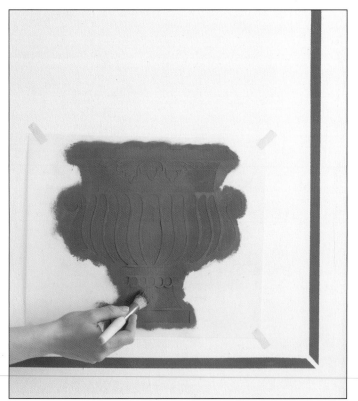

6 Using spray mount, stick one urn stencil within the frame. Paint a thin coat of mid-blue paint on to the tile. Dab at the paint with the stencil brush and stencil the urn. Leave to dry.

7 Blend mid-blue and pale blue paint together and then shade the centre of the urn to highlight the urn and create its rounded appearance. Leave to dry and remove the stencil.

RENAISSANCE HALLWAY

Turn your hallway into a dramatic entrance with ornate stencils and rich lustrous colours. Combine them with gold accessories, velvets and braids to complete the theatrical and luxurious setting. This design would also be ideal for creating an intimate atmosphere in a dining room, perfect for candlelit dinners.

You will need

- ruler
- spirit level
- pencil
- masking tape
- emulsion (latex) paints in pale slate-blue, terracotta and pale peach
- large household sponge
- stencil brushes
- stencil card
- craft knife and self-healing cutting mat
- stencil paints in dark grey-blue, terracotta, emerald and turquoise

1 Using a ruler and spirit level, divide the wall in half horizontally with a pencil line, then draw a second line 15cm/6in above the first. Stick a line of masking tape just below this top line. Dilute one part slate-blue emulsion (latex) paint with one part water and colour the top half of the wall using a household sponge.

2 Stick masking tape just above the bottom pencil line. Dilute one part terracotta emulsion paint with one part water and sponge over the lower half of the wall.

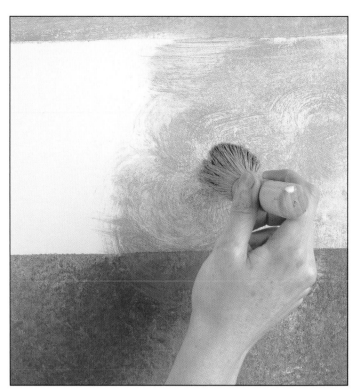

3 Sponge lightly over the terracotta paint with slate-blue emulsion (latex) paint to add a textural effect. Remove the strips of masking tape once you have covered the whole of the wall.

4 Colour the centre band with diluted peach emulsion, using a stencil brush. Trace the templates at the back of the book and cut out the stencils from stencil card using a craft knife and cutting mat.

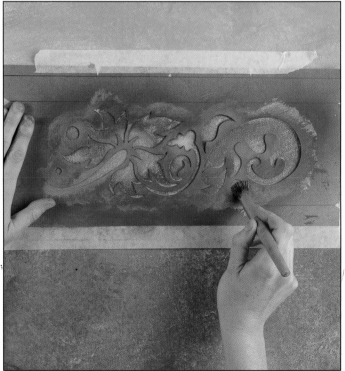

5 Stencil the wall motifs at roughly regular intervals over the upper part of the wall, using dark grey-blue stencil paint, keeping the brush upright and moving it in a circular motion. Rotate the stencil with every alternate motif to give movement to the design.

6 Starting at the right-hand side of the peach band, stencil the border motif with terracotta stencil paint. Add details in emerald and turquoise. Continue along the wall, positioning the stencil beside the previous motif so that the spaces are equal, creating a balanced effect.

FOLK ART WALL

This combination of border patterns and larger single motifs is typical of the stencil designs used by the itinerant painters who worked in the American colonies in the early 19th century. There was little anxiety about whether patterns turned the corners accurately, it was the harmonious colour schemes that made the result so successful.

You will need

- acetate sheet
- craft knife and self-healing cutting mat
- spray mount
- stencil paint in brick red and dull green
- two stencil brushes
- plumbline

ABOVE: This door was painted but you could easily stencil heart motifs instead.

1 Enlarge the templates at the back of the book on a photocopier. Cut out from acetate sheet using a craft knife and cutting mat. Spray the border stencil lightly with spray mount and align it with either the picture or the dado (chair) rail.

2 Begin stencilling the border design, using a separate stencil brush for each colour.

3 If your stencil is an acetate sheet you will be able to see where the second stencil meets the first; if you are using stencil card place it above the first and lift the bottom corner to check that it is in position.

4 Turn the stencil to make the border panels, using a plumbline from the ceiling in order to check the borders are aligned. Repeat this process to frame the room with as many stencilled panels as you need.

5 Using dull green paint, stencil the willow trees in the centre of the panels, one above the other, keeping the stencil brush upright and moving it in a circular motion. The tree looks best with a bit of space all around it.

PENNSYLVANIA DUTCH TULIPS

This American folk art inspired idea uses the rich colours and simple motifs beloved by the German and Dutch immigrants to Pennsylvania. Create the effect of all-over handpainted wallpaper or, for a beginner's project, take a single motif and use it to decorate a cabinet, a chest of drawers or the top of a wooden chest.

You will need

- dark ochre emulsion (latex) paint
- large and small decorator's paintbrushes
- woodwash in indigo blue and mulberry
- tracing paper
- stencil card
- craft knife and self-healing cutting mat
- ruler
- pencil
- masking tape
- stencil brushes
- stencil paints in red, light green, dark green and pale brown
- clean cotton rag
- artist's brush

1 Dilute one part ochre emulsion (latex) paint with one part water. Using a large decorator's paintbrush, cover the top half of the wall. Use vertical brushstrokes for an even texture.

2 Paint the lower half of the wall, underneath the dado (chair) rail if there is one, with indigo blue woodwash. Finish with a curving line using a dry brush to suggest woodgrain.

3 Using a small decorator's paintbrush, paint the dado rail or a strip at dado-rail height in mulberry woodwash.

4 Trace the tulip and heart template from the back of the book. Cut the stencils from stencil card using a craft knife and cutting mat. Mark the centre of each edge of the stencil. Measure the wall and divide it into equal sections, so that the repeats will fall at about 20cm/8in intervals. Mark the positions lightly in pencil, so they can be erased later.

5 Tape the first stencil in position using low-tack masking tape. Dip a medium stencil brush into red stencil paint. Rub the brush on a white tile, saucer or rag until it is almost dry before stencilling in the tulips. Leave to dry.

6 Paint the leaves in light green stencil paint with darker green shading. Paint the stems in dark green using a fine stencil brush. Leave to dry.

Stencil a single heart between the two baskets of tulips using a very little red stencil paint.

7 Lightly stencil the tulip basket in pale brown stencil paint using a chunky stencil brush and a small amount of paint.

RIGHT: Decorate a matching key cupboard or storage box following the same method and using just one motif in the centre. You could alter the colour of the tulips if you so wish.

OPPOSITE: These vibrant colours will instantly lift a dull hallway, bringing a touch of spring into your home with the use of a charming floral theme.

PAISLEY PATTERN WALL

The paisley or pine motif originated in India, where it has been used in painted, woven and embroidered decoration for centuries. This interpretation in soft earthy tones could be used for a living or dining room in either a traditional or contemporary setting.

1 Paint the wall with one or two coats of pale terracotta emulsion (latex) paint, depending on the density of colour you require. Leave to dry.

2 Cut a rectangle of paper 30 x 40cm/ 12 x 16in. With a soft pencil, lightly pencil a grid across the wall drawing along the sides of the paper.

3 Enlarge the template at the back of the book on a photocopier. Transfer on to stencil card using carbon paper. Cut out using a craft knife and cutting mat, and transfer the registration marks. Draw a central cross on each, dividing it into quarters, then cut a notch at the end of each line. Spray the outline stencil with spray mount and line it up on the wall, matching the notches to the pencilled grid. Tape it down and draw in the registration marks.

OPPOSITE: The colours used in this enduring motif can be adapted to suit a room of your choice such as a study or hallway.

4 Using a large stencil brush, fill in the outline with cream paint, using a heavy stippling. Leave to dry.

▶

5 Fill in the remaining space with more paisley shapes, placing one in every other space in a half-drop or brick arrangement.

6 Using the registration marks and grid as a guide, tape the second stencil in place over the paisley outline once the paint has dried.

7 Using a smaller stencil brush and turquoise acrylic paint, stipple all over the design. Work in light strokes across the background shape.

8 Add a light stippling of terracotta paint over the central part of each motif.

9 Fill in the rest of the paisley motifs in the same way. Any variation in colour will add interest and authenticity to the design.

10 Lightly paint a terracotta detail stencil in each remaining space, positioning the paisley the other way up. Erase all the pencil marks. If the wall is in an area where it will receive a lot of wear and tear, spray with two coats of matt (flat) varnish to protect the stencils.

LEAFY FIREPLACE SURROUND

This row of stylized leaves turns a plain fireplace into a bold design statement and adds an element of pattern to an otherwise plain wall. Adapt the size and number of the motifs to suit the width of your mantelpiece.

You will need

- carbon paper
- sharp pencil
- stencil card
- craft knife and self-healing cutting mat
- ruler
- soft pencil
- set square (triangle)
- stencil brush
- dark green stencil paint
- eraser

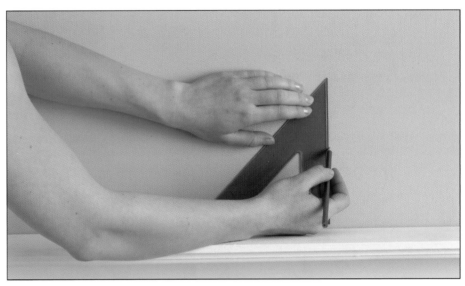

1 Enlarge the template at the back of the book and trace it on to stencil card. Using a craft knife and cutting mat cut it out, leaving a 3cm/1¼in border at each side edge and a 1cm/½in border along the bottom. Draw in a vertical line along the centre of the leaf. Using soft pencil, lightly draw a vertical line to mark the centre of the fireplace. Decide how far above the mantelpiece you wish the border to be and draw a horizontal line at this height.

2 Line up the middle of the stencil along the centre point with the bottom edge on the horizontal line.

3 Stipple in the first leaf using a large stencil brush. Apply the paint in a slightly uneven way to give texture to the motif: stipple two coats, if necessary, to create the desired effect.

4 To space the leaves regularly, position the stencil so that the right-hand edge of the card almost touches the left-hand edge of the previous leaf.

5 Continue stencilling a row of leaves towards the left-hand end of the mantlepiece, then work towards the right-hand edge in the same way. Make sure that the motifs are all spaced evenly and that the design is symmetrical.

6 Mark the position of the final leaf on the left by drawing a guideline downwards from the outside edge of the last stencil. Decide how far down you wish the leaf to be – this will be roughly half the height of the leaf, depending on the shape of the fireplace.

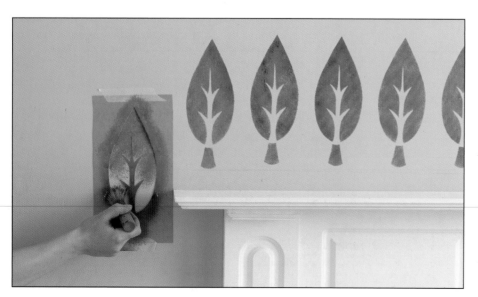

7 Stencil in the leaf. Repeat at the right-hand end, making sure that the two final leaves are at the same height. Erase the pencil mark. For a more subtle look you could paint the leaves in a more pastel shade of green, or use an autumnal deep red or brown for a warmer effect.

OPPOSITE: *The fresh green leaves make a good contrast against the soft green background wall.*

ELEGANT ROSE TREE

Create a dramatic effect on a wall with this beautiful and elegant rose tree. Full-bloom roses, buds and leaves are stencilled along the painted branches. The tree can be worked as large or small as you wish. The background wall was painted in soft pink emulsion (latex) but you can adapt this colour if you so wish.

OPPOSITE: A dusky pink background tones well with the warm colours of the tree.

1 Trace the rose, leaves and bud templates from the back of the book. Tape to the stencil card and cut out using a craft knife and cutting mat. Use a soft pencil to very lightly draw a trunk and branches for the rose tree on the wall.

2 ▼ Using a medium artist's brush, paint the trunk along the pencil lines with brown acrylic paint.

▶

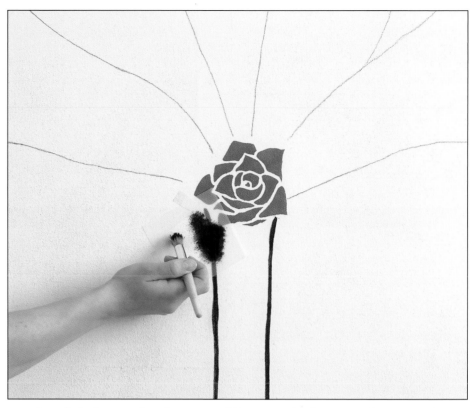

3 Tape the rose stencil to the wall at the top of the trunk. If the rose covers the pencil lines, gently rub them away with an eraser. Apply a thin coat of dusky pink paint to a ceramic tile with a flat paintbrush. Dab at the paint with a stencil brush and stencil the rose, holding the stencil brush upright and moving it in a circular motion.

4 Stencil the leaves a few times around the rose using brown acrylic paint and a small stencil brush.

5 The rose, leaves and bud stencils are worked outwards along the branches from the first rose. As you work, erase any pencil lines that will be covered by the stencils. Blend dusky pink and purple paint together on the tile for the buds.

6 Continue stencilling the roses, leaves and buds along the branches. Apply some leaves singly, masking the surrounding leaves on the stencil with card to protect them from any splashes of paint.

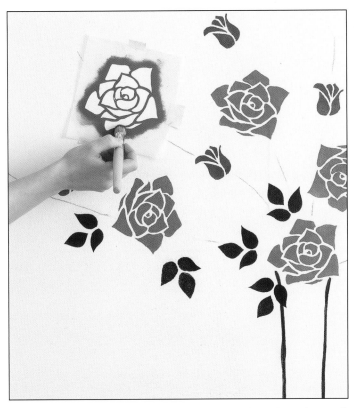

7 Apply the stencils to the outer reaches of the branches and continue the stencilling.

8 Stencil leaves or buds at the ends of the branches using card to protect the roses.

9 Stencil single leaves in any of the gaps, masking the surrounding leaves as before. Using the medium artist's brush, carefully paint in the branches, radiating outwards from the trunk.

10 Add a few stems to the leaves with brown paint using the medium artist's brush. Stand back from the tree to see if there are any obvious gaps that could be filled with a bud or leaves and then stencil them in place.

JAPANESE ORANGE BLOSSOM WALL

Inspired by delicate Japanese silk hangings, this blossom and bamboo design is made up from two versatile stencils, which can be adapted and rearranged in an endless variety of ways to fill any space, from a small recess to an entire wall.

You will need

- masking tape
- large sheet of acetate
- sheet of glass
- heat knife
- spray mount
- stencil brushes
- acrylic paints in pale jade, dark green, light brown, apricot and pink

1 Enlarge the templates at the back of the book and make up the acetate. Spray the back of the bamboo stencil lightly with spray mount and tape in place. Lightly stipple the whole motif in pale jade paint.

2 Add a little dark green paint to the jade acrylic paint and mix the colours thoroughly. Stipple the ends of the leaves with a light, tapping action to give depth to the shape and a three-dimensional look.

3 Using a fine brush and a small amound of paint stencil a light brown layer over the green stems. Do the same on each stem across the design.

4 Stencil one or more additional branch designs around the first, using the same colours. You can use parts of the stencil to fill in smaller areas.

5 Fix the blossom stencil in position and stipple in the stems with jade green paint. Add a darker colour along the edges as before.

6 Using a soft brush, stencil in the flowers and buds using apricot paint. Be careful not to overload the brush to maintain a delicate effect.

7 Add soft pink shading to the outer edges of the blossom flowers and the buds to give them a three-dimensional look.

8 Choose part of the bamboo stencil to add further foliage to the motifs and stipple in the design as before, using the same colours.

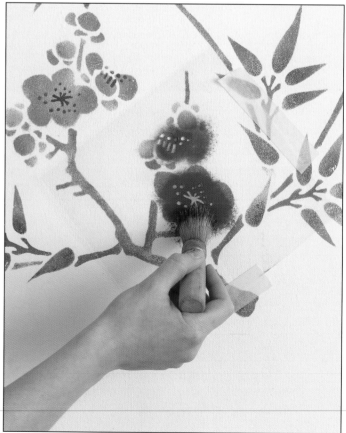

9 Single flowers or small sprigs can be added using parts of the blossom motif. Mask off the parts of the stencil that are not being used with tape, if necessary.

10 Using the dark green paint and the third stencil, add the stamens to the blossom flowers. Vary the angle of the stencil for each group of flowers.

STAR BATHROOM

This misty blue colour scheme is ideal for a bathroom or staircase because the lower part of the wall is varnished to provide a practical wipe-clean surface. The tinted varnish deepens the colour and gives it a sheen that contrasts well with the chalky distemper (tempera) paint above. The star is a traditional quilting motif.

You will need

- tracing paper and pen
- scissors
- spray mount
- stencil card
- craft knife and self-healing cutting mat
- soft blue distemper (tempera) paint or chalk-based paint
- large decorator's paintbrushes
- straightedge
- spirit level
- soft pencil
- clear satin water-based varnish and brush
- Prussian blue artist's acrylic paint

1 Trace the star template from the back of the book and cut out. Lightly spray the back with spray mount and stick to the stencil card.

2 Cut out the star using a craft knife and cutting mat. Cut inwards from the points towards the centre so that the points stay crisp.

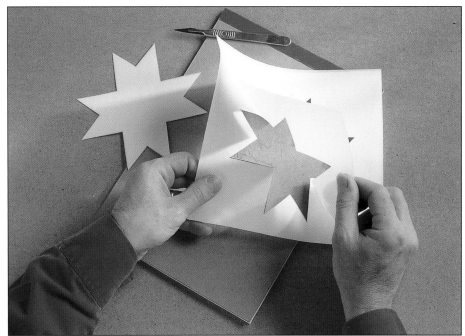

3 Taking a corner first, carefully peel away the paper template on the top to reveal the stencil underneath.

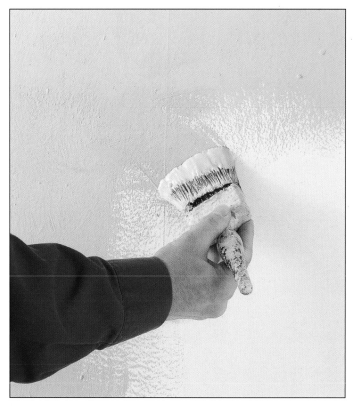

4 Dilute the paint, if necessary, according to the manufacturer's instructions. Brush it onto the wall with sweeping, random strokes to give a colourwashed effect.

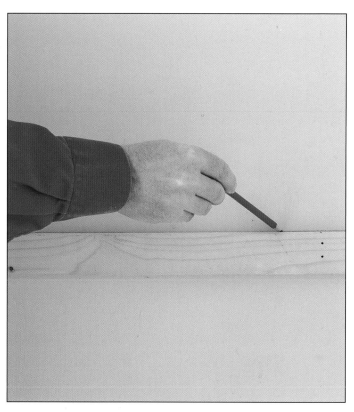

5 Using a straightedge and spirit level, draw a pencil line across the wall at the height you want to end the darker varnished surface.

6 Tint the satin water-based varnish with a squeeze of Prussian blue acrylic paint. Using a separate decorator's brush, apply this on the lower part of the wall up to the marked line.

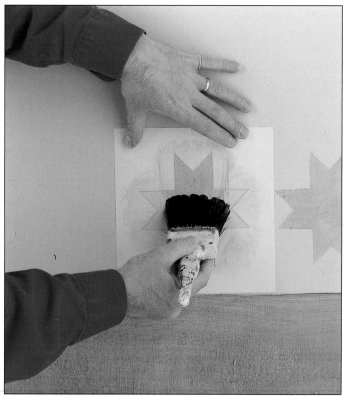

7 Spray the back of the stencil with spray mount and position at one end of the wall, 5cm/2in above the marked line. Stencil with the tinted varnish, using a broad sweep of the brush. Repeat along the wall, spacing the stars evenly.

BATHROOM FRIEZE

Create a mosaic border on a tiled splashback using ceramic paints, available from art and craft shops. The mosaic design works well as a frieze because the narrow silver bands match up to create continuous lines flowing across the tiles.

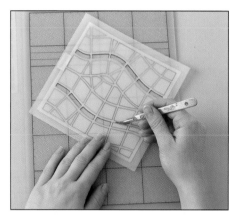

1 Trace the template at the back of the book. Tape the tracing to a piece of stencil card. Using a craft knife and cutting mat, cut out the stencils along the solid outer lines. You will need two stencils – the mosaics and the silver bands.

2 Spray the back of the mosaic stencil with spray mount. Stick it to a tile, matching the outer edges and smoothing the stencil outwards from the centre. Stick masking tape around the outer edges to protect the surrounding area from paint.

3 Using a flat paintbrush, spread a thin coat of blue paint on to a spare tile. Dab at the paint with a stencil brush and stencil the mosaics holding the stencil brush perpendicular to the tiles and moving it in a circular motion. Leave to dry then remove the stencil.

4 Spray the back of the silver bands stencil with spray mount. Stick it to the tile, matching the outer edges. Mask off the surrounding area at the ends of the bands with masking tape. Stencil the bands with silver paint. Leave to dry. Repeat on the remaining tiles.

MAKING SANDCASTLES

Evocative of childhood summers spent on the beach, sandcastles are simple, colourful shapes to stencil. Perfect for a child's room or for a bathroom, they will bring a touch of humour to your walls. Instead of stencilling the flags you can glue on paper flags for added interest.

You will need

- emulsion (latex) paints in blue and white
- decorator's paintbrush
- household sponge
- acetate sheet
- craft knife and self-healing cutting mat
- tape measure
- soft pencil
- masking tape
- stencil paints in yellow, black and other colours of your choice
- stencil brushes
- fine artist's paint brush
- coloured paper (optional)
- PVA (white) glue (optional)

1 Paint below the dado (chair) rail height in blue emulsion (latex) paint. When dry, lightly rub on white emulsion with a sponge. Trace the templates at the back of the book. Cut the stencils from an acetate sheet using a craft knife and cutting mat.

2 Measure the wall to calculate how many sandcastles you can fit on and make very light marks with a soft pencil at regular intervals. Hold the stencil above the dado rail and secure the corners with low-tack masking tape.

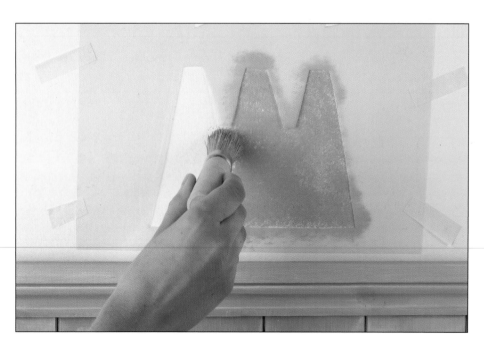

3 Using the yellow stencil paint and a thick stencil brush, stencil in the first sandcastle. Repeat for the other sandcastles.

OPPOSITE: Vary the colours of the central stars and the flags but work within a chosen colour palette.

4 Stencil each flag in a different colour of your choice.

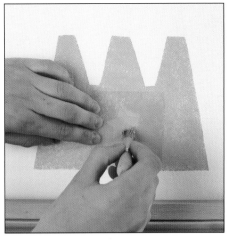

5 When the paint has dried, stencil a star on each sandcastle in a contrasting colour of paint.

6 Using a fine artist's paintbrush and black stencil paint, carefully paint in the flagpoles.

7 Continue stencilling the sandcastles along the wall, using your pencil marks to position them.

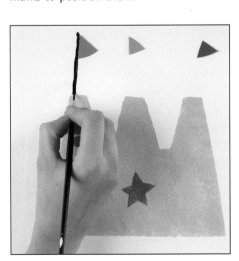

8 As an alternative to stencilling the flags, cut triangles of coloured paper and glue them to the wall with PVA (white) glue, then paint in the flagpoles.

FLAG STENCILS

This strong graphic design will add colour and fun to a child's room or a study. The easiest way to make a stencil is to photocopy a simple motif on to acetate sheet. Here, two complementary flag motifs are combined. Use the stencils as a border at picture or dado (chair) rail height, randomly around the room or in straight lines to make a feature of, for example, an alcove on one wall.

1 Photocopy the designs from the back of the book at various sizes until you are happy with the size. Photocopy them directly on to the acetate sheet.

2 Cut out the stencils using a craft knife and cutting mat.

OPPOSITE: Bold and primary colours have been used here and work well on a plain white background. You could soften the effect by using pastels if you wish.

3 Tape the stencils to the wall using masking tape, alternating the flags and the direction they are facing. Stencil a bold outline in black.

4 Use a medium stencil brush to apply the colour inside the outlines, or paint it freehand for a looser, more childlike effect.

CHILD'S SEASIDE ROOM

This pretty frieze shows a jaunty crab, a starfish and a scallop shell riding on the crest of a wave stencilled along a practical peg rail. A small co-ordinating mirror bordered with little fishes and a wave completes the effect. Use sea-inspired colours such as blue, aquamarine or pale coral as here or choose your own colour palette.

You will need

- tracing paper and pen
- masking tape
- stencil card
- craft knife and self-healing cutting mat
- small decorator's paintbrush
- wooden peg rail
- pale blue emulsion (latex) paint
- flat paintbrush
- acrylic paints in aquamarine, turquoise, dark coral and pale coral
- ceramic tile
- stencil brush
- spirit level
- soft pencil
- eraser
- wooden framed mirror
- fine-grade abrasive paper (optional)
- damp rag (optional)
- sheet of paper

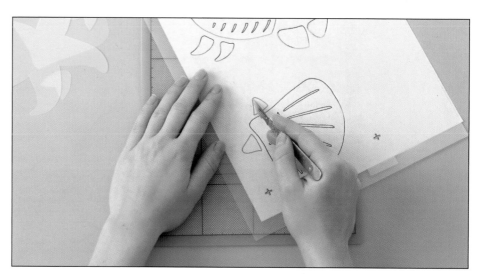

1 Trace the templates at the back of the book. Tape a piece of stencil card to the tracings. Using a craft knife and cutting mat, cut out the stencils. You will need two stencils for the frieze – the starfish, crab and shell, and the details.

2 Remove the pegs from the peg rail. Paint the peg rail with pale blue emulsion (latex) paint. Leave to dry. Tape the waves stencil to the top of the peg rail at one end. Using a flat paintbrush, spread a thin coat of aquamarine and turquoise acrylic paints on to a ceramic tile. Dab at the paints with a stencil brush and stencil the wave, blending the colours together at random.

3 Leave to dry completely then remove the stencil. Move the stencil along the peg rail, matching the valley of the waves so the stencil appears to "flow" seamlessly, and continue stencilling.

4 Use the stencil brush to paint the ends and lower edge of the peg rail to match the waves using a flat paintbrush blending the colours together at random as before. Fix the pegs in place. Paint the pegs with dark coral paint.

5 Using a spirit level, lightly mark the position of the peg rail on the wall with a soft pencil. Tape the starfish, crab and shell stencil to the wall above the peg rail position. Stencil the cut-outs with dark coral paint and leave to dry.

6 Stencil the centre of the starfish, crab and shell with pale coral acrylic paint.

7 Lightly shade the edges of the crab stencil with aquamarine acrylic paint. Leave to dry completely then carefully remove the stencil.

8 Tape the stencils of the details to the wall, matching up the registration marks. Stencil the details with turquoise paint. Leave them to dry then erase the pencil marks. Fix the peg rail to the wall matching the top edge of the peg rail to the drawn pencil line.

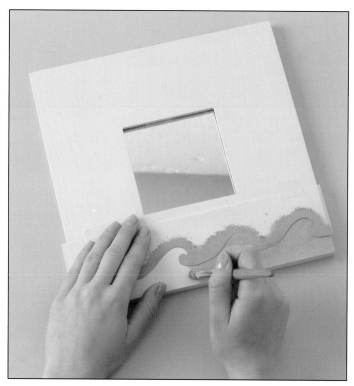

9 If your wooden mirror frame is varnished or already painted, sand it first with fine-grade abrasive paper then wipe it clean with a damp rag. Slip pieces of paper under the edges framing the mirror to protect it from any splashes of paint. Paint the frame with pale blue emulsion paint. Leave to dry.

10 Tape the waves stencil across the bottom of the frame. Using the flat paintbrush, spread a thin coat of aquamarine and turquoise paint on the ceramic tile. Dab at the paints with the stencil brush and stencil the wave, blending the colours together on the frame. Use the stencil brush to paint the lower edges of the frame to match the waves.

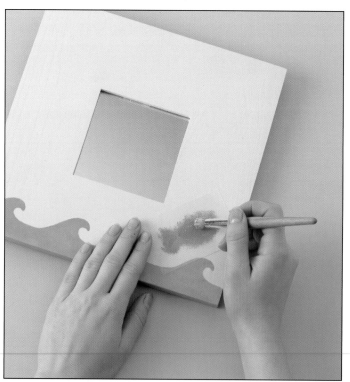

11 Tape the fish stencil to the frame above the waves. Stencil the fish with dark coral paint. Leave to dry.

12 Lightly shade the fish with aquamarine paint. Stencil more fish at random on the frame.

ANIMAL BEDROOM

Small children like the security of enclosed sleeping spaces and older children relish the privacy, especially if their room is shared with a brother or sister. The panels can be attached to the bed base or simply rested in a corner so that they enclose the space but cannot be pushed over. The animal stencils can also be used on the walls.

1 The shorter pieces of chipboard (particle board) are used for the head and foot of the bed. Screw the batten (furring strip) to butt up to one 1.2m/2ft edge of the head and foot pieces. Place the long piece of chipboard up against the batten on the headboard, at right angles, and screw in place. Repeat with the foot, to make a three-sided surround for the bed. The bed surround will now be reasonably stable, but it is advisable to position the long side against a wall. Paint the surround with pale grey emulsion (latex) paint.

2 To stencil the bed linen, enlarge the templates from the back of the book on a photocopier. Coat the backs lightly with spray mount and stick them on to stencil card.

3 Cut out the stencils using a craft knife and self-healing cutting mat.

4 Wash and iron the sheet and pillowcase. Place some paper inside the pillowcase to protect the back. Position the first stencil, holding it in place with masking tape.

5 Spread each of the fabric paints on to a plate. Using a stencil brush, dab the first colour on to the pillowcase. Apply the paint sparingly because the colour is best when built up gradually.

6 Position the next stencil, being very careful not to smudge the first one, and then stencil the second animal in another colour.

7 Position a third stencil and apply the final colour. Continue alternating the stencils and colours. Decorate the top of the sheet in the same way.

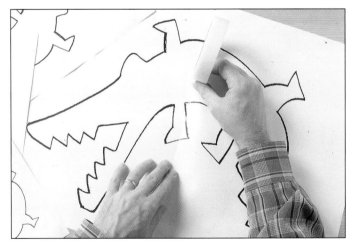

8 To make the "window", enlarge the crocodile template at the back of the book in sections so that you end up with a large pattern. Tape the sections together.

9 Rub the back of the pattern outline with a soft pencil.

10 Place the pattern face up on the chipboard and draw over the outline with a hard pencil. Drill a hole at any point on the outline as the insertion point for the jigsaw (saber saw) blade.

11 Cut out the crocodile shape, working slowly and holding the blade vertically so that it cuts at its own speed without being dragged through the chipboard.

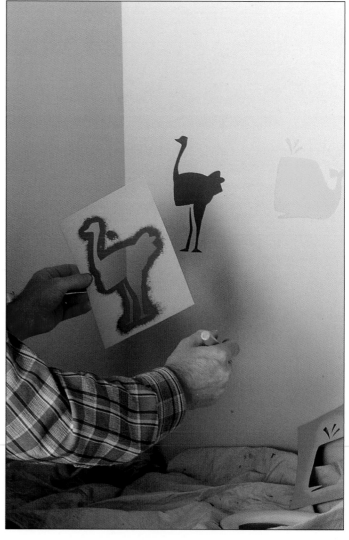

12 Rub down all the edges of the cut-out crocodile shape using fine-grade abrasive paper to smooth the edges and remove any burrs.

13 Stencil a frieze of animals around the bed screen, using the fabric paints or matching stencil paints.

OPPOSITE: You can use the animal stencils to decorate walls, borders and friezes, bed linen and wash bags to create a co-ordinated room scheme.

BRIGHT TRANSPORT BORDER

Any small child keen on cars, vans and trucks would love to have these vehicles making their way around the bedroom walls. Complete the theme by stencilling a favourite car on a co-ordinating bag.

You will need

- tracing paper and pen
- 12mm/½in wide masking tape
- stencil card
- craft knife and self-healing cutting mat
- metal ruler
- spirit level
- flat paintbrush
- acrylic paints in grey, blue, lilac, lime green, pink and yellow
- ceramic tile
- stencil brush
- soft pencil
- eraser
- plastic bag
- ready-made fabric bag
- fabric marking pen
- fabric paints in pink, blue and yellow
- iron

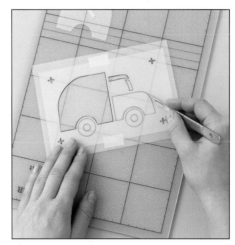

1 Trace the templates at the back of the book. Tape a piece of stencil card to the tracings. Using a craft knife and cutting mat cut out the stencils, cutting straight lines against a metal ruler. You will need three stencils for each vehicle – the wheels, the body and the hub caps.

2 Stick a length of low-tack masking tape across the wall to designate the road, using a spirit level to check that it is straight. When positioning the road, remember to allow space above for the cars and trucks.

3 Stick lengths of tape immediately above and below the first tape. Peel off the first tape. Do not discard it but cut it into approximate 4cm/1½in lengths. Stick the pieces vertically across the road 8cm/3¼in apart to create a broken line. Alternatively, leave the line unbroken if you prefer.

4 Using a flat paintbrush, spread a thin coat of grey paint on to a ceramic tile. Dab at the paint with a stencil brush and stencil the road. Leave the paint to dry then carefully pull off all the masking tape.

5 Tape the wheels stencil to the wall, placing the lower registration marks on the upper edge of the road. Mark the top registration marks and the top strut of the lower registration marks with a soft pencil.

6 Spread a thin coat of blue acrylic paint on the ceramic tile. Dab at the paint with the stencil brush and stencil the wheels. Leave to dry. Remove the stencil then tape the vehicle body stencil in place, matching the registration marks. Stencil the vehicle body using lilac paint.

7 Leave to dry completely. Remove the stencil then tape the hub cap stencil in place, matching up with the registration marks. Stencil the hub caps with yellow acrylic paint. Leave to dry then remove the stencil. The first vehicle is now complete.

8 Move the stencils along the wall, matching the right-hand registration marks of the previous vehicle with the left-hand registration marks of the next. Stencil the vehicles in different colours and avoid having the same type of vehicles end to end. Leave to dry, remove the stencils then gently erase the registration marks.

9 Slide a plastic bag inside the fabric bag to prevent paint seeping through to the back. Tape the wheels stencil of one of the vehicles to the bag 6cm/2¹⁄₂in above the lower edge. Mark the registration marks with a fabric marking pen. Using the flat paintbrush spread a thin coat of pink fabric paint on to the tile. Dab at the paint with the stencil brush and stencil the wheels. Leave to dry.

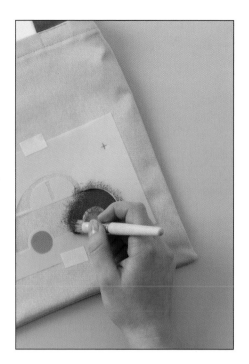

10 Remove the stencil then tape the vehicle body stencil in place, matching the registration marks. Stencil the vehicle using blue fabric paint. Leave to dry. Remove the stencil then tape the hub cap stencil in place, matching the registration marks. Stencil the hub caps with yellow fabric paint. Leave to dry then remove the stencil. Pull the plastic bag partly out to protect the work surface under the handles of the bag.

11 Stick masking tape along each edge of one handle, leaving a 1cm/¹/₂in gap, and tape over the ends of the handle. Lay a section of the handle out flat, then stencil along the masked line with yellow fabric paint.

12 Leave to dry completely then lay the next section flat and continue stencilling. Peel off the tape when the paint has dried. Repeat to stencil the other handle in the same way. Iron the bag on the wrong side to fix (set) the paint, following the manufacturer's instructions.

RIGHT: Use the stencils of the cars, vans and trucks to decorate items in a child's room such as walls, borders and bags to create a co-ordinated scheme.

VICTORIAN WINDOW

This idea originated from the etched-glass windows of the Victorian era. The paint needs to be sprayed very lightly, so practise on some picture frame glass first to judge the effect. The stencil design is provided at the back of the book, but you could easily design your own. Look at examples of lace panels to get some inspiration.

OPPOSITE: This simple, but effective, method can be used in bathrooms or closets.

1 Measure the window panes, and mark the halfway points with masking tape. Trace the stencil design at the back of the book and cut out from stencil card using a craft knife and cutting mat.

2 Tape the main stencil pattern in position. Then use brown wrapping paper to mask off the surrounding area, at least 50cm/20in deep on all sides. (The spray spreads more than you think.)

3 Follow the paint manufacturer's instructions and shake the can for as long as needed, since this affects the fineness of the spray. Spray from a distance of at least 30cm/12in.

4 Depending on the dimensions of the window panes, there may be strips along the sides of the main panel that also need stencilling. This pattern has a border to fit around the edge.

ART NOUVEAU TILES

These elegant and highly stylized designs are inspired by the work of Scottish artist Charles Rennie Mackintosh and the Glasgow School of Art at the turn of the 20th century.

1 Enlarge the designs at the back of the book on a photocopier to fit your tiles. Cut two pieces of stencil card to the size of the tiles and transfer one design to each. Cut away the centre of each design using a craft knife and cutting mat. Coat the back of the stencils with spray mount. Place the stem stencil on a tile. Using a dry artist's brush, apply dark green paint to the stems and light green to the leaves.

2 Allow the paint to dry completely, then use a clean, dry brush to add a little deep red paint to pick out the thorns on the stem. You might also like to try reversing the stem stencil on some of the tiles, which will make the overall effect more symmetrical.

3 Mix deep red with white ceramic paint to make a dusky pink shade. Using this colour and a dry paintbrush, stencil the rose motif on to another tile. Leave the paint to dry completely.

4 Add deep red around the edges of the petals to emphasize the rose shape and give it depth.

BELOW: This design could be adapted to create a stylized border.

5 Using a fine artist's brush, add a few green dots in the centre of the rose. Leave to dry, then seal the surface of the tiles with two coats of varnish, allowing them to dry between coats.

MEDALLION STENCILLED FLOOR

In America, floor stencilling began in imitation of expensive Oriental rugs. Some early Pennsylvania Dutch houses used oak flooring, but more usually floorboards were of pine painted with many layers of oil paint to prevent it from splintering, and then stencilled with intricate colourful borders and repeat patterns.

You will need

- sugar soap or all-purpose cleaner
- olive green matt emulsion (flat latex) paint
- two medium-sized household paintbrushes
- clean cotton rag (optional)
- stencil brush
- tape measure or ruler
- acetate sheet or stencil card
- craft knife and cutting mat
- spray mount
- black matt emulsion or stencil paint
- masking tape
- hard-wearing polyurethane varnish

OPPOSITE: This design could be used to create a simple border pattern on the floor.

1 Prepare the surface by washing with sugar soap or all-purpose cleaner. When dry, paint with green emulsion (latex) paint. If you like a worn-looking surface thin the emulsion half and half with water and wipe it on with a rag. The paint will stay in the grain and give a patchy effect. Leave to dry.

2 Measure the floor space to judge how many medallions will fit easily between each corner. Enlarge the template at the back of the book and cut out of acetate or card using a craft knife and cutting mat. Spray lightly with spray mount. Begin by stencilling a medallion in each corner then one midway between the two. Continue stencilling alternate sides of the central medallion, spacing by eye until you reach the corner motif.

3 Stencil one row of medallions all around the room first, to act as a guide when positioning the other rows. The grid of large medallions can be broken up by using the centre of the motif between each block of four. Use masking tape to isolate the centre and make a smaller stencil to fill in the gaps. Finally paint the floor surface with two or three coats of varnish.

GREEK KEY FLOOR BORDER

Classic patterns have a timeless air, which makes them suitable for a formal room scheme. This geometric pattern is derived from the border on an Ancient Greek vase. It consists of two simple motifs, which can be stencilled in straight lines or around corners.

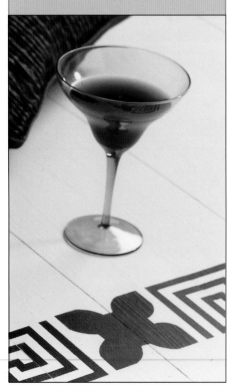

OPPOSITE: Bold shapes and strong geometric patterns work well on painted white or light-coloured floorboards.

1 Prepare the floor by sanding down the boards, then painting them with white floor paint. If the floor has already been painted, wash it down with a soft cloth to remove any dust, grease and marks. If you wish, you can also sand it lightly to key the surface.

2 Enlarge the templates at the back of the book on a photocopier to the size required and tape on to stencil card. Cut out and trim the border to 1cm/½in all round. Starting from one corner of the room, position the stencil in the centre of a floorboard.

3 Tape the stencil in position. While you are stencilling, hold a piece of card (stock) over the edge of the stencil to protect the floor from surplus paint or splashes.

4 Load the stencil brush very lightly with black paint and block in the design, using two coats if necessary for a dense look. When dry, lift the stencil and remove the tape.

5 Line up the stencil so that one short edge lies against the painted design and one long edge lies against the masking tape. Tape the two long edges in place, avoiding any already painted areas, then fill in the stencil as before.

6 Continue stencilling to the end of the wall. Start the next side of the floor border by lining up the stencil at right angles to the first motif. Use a set square (triangle) as you work to ensure the border is straight.

7 Repeat on the other two sides using the set square to make sure that each corner is at a right angle. Leave to dry then apply three coats of clear, heavy-duty matt (flat) varnish to seal the floor and protect it from hard wear.

FURNITURE AND STORAGE

S tencilling is a quick and effective way to revive an old piece of furniture or flea market find, or to add decoration to a plain flat-pack chest of drawers or table. Take the time to sand and prime the wood before you start for the best results, and don't be put off by working on a larger scale: start off with a smaller item such as a key cabinet and then progress to tables, chairs and shelving.

ABOVE: Old-fashioned style trains and carriages are popular themes for children's rooms and storage.

LEFT: Smarten up a simple kitchen chair with delicate Scandinavian-style stencilling.

BRONZE CHAIR

This handsome gilded design was inspired by the high-quality "Hitchcock" chairs popular in America in the 19th century, named after the man who mass-produced them. The brilliance of the colour comes from real bronze powder (or gold powder, which is more expensive), and the effect is quite different to bronze or gold paint, or bronze or gold leaf. The original makers used the finest velvet to apply the powder, moulding the shapes of fruit and flowers by varying the amount of powder.

You will need

- kitchen chair with broad rails and turned legs (or plain pine rocking chair)
- fine-grade abrasive paper
- clean cotton rag
- black emulsion (latex) paint
- small decorator's paintbrush
- spray mount
- stencil card
- craft knife and self-healing cutting mat
- water-based gold size
- plate
- stencil brush
- bronze or gold powder
- square of lint or velvet
- fine artist's brush
- antiquing varnish (or clear satin varnish) and brush

1 Rub down any existing paintwork with abrasive paper.

2 Dust off the surface with a clean cotton rag.

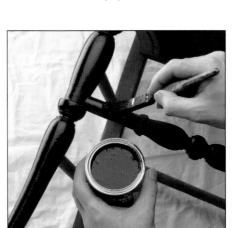

3 Paint the chair with black emulsion (latex) paint.

OPPOSITE: The stencil for this chair is very intricate and will take time to cut out.

4 Photocopy the stencil pattern at the back of the book, enlarging it to fit your chair back. Spray the back of the pattern with spray mount and stick it on to stencil card. Cut out the small shapes using a craft knife and cutting mat.

5 Complete cutting out the pattern, then cut away the extra card so that the stencil fits your chair back. Lay the stencil in position on the chair back.

6 Place a small amount of size on a plate. Using a stencil brush, stipple the size through the shapes. Use the size sparingly, but fill in each shape.

7 When the size is just tacky (see manufacturer's instructions), dust on bronze or gold powder. Work it into the size by applying it with a piece of lint or velvet.

8 Leave the bronze or gold powder for 1–2 hours to set. Gently wipe away any excess with a small square of lint or soft velvet.

9 Highlight details on the rest of the chair. Apply size with a fine artist's brush, then add the bronze or gold powder. If desired, you can soften the gold effect with a coat of antiquing varnish, which will also protect the stencilling. Clear satin varnish will give protection without dulling the gold.

SCANDINAVIAN CHAIR

These motifs can be adjusted to fit any style of wooden chair, which can be decorated as simply or lavishly as you wish. Here, white paint is applied to a blue chair but other combinations such as red paint on a white chair would also look good.

You will need

- tracing paper and pen
- carbon paper
- stencil card
- masking tape
- sharp pencil
- craft knife and self-healing cutting mat
- metal ruler
- flat paintbrush
- white acrylic paint
- ceramic tile
- stencil brush

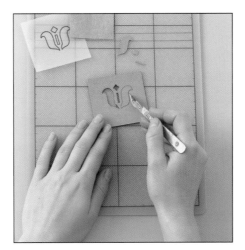

1 Trace the templates at the back of the book. Place a piece of carbon paper face down on to a sheet of stencil card. Tape the tracings on top. Redraw the templates with a sharp pencil to transfer the design. Using a sharp-bladed craft knife and cutting mat cut out the stencils, cutting straight lines against a metal ruler.

2 Tape the large star flower stencil centrally on to the chair seat. Using a flat paintbrush, spread a thin coat of white paint on to a ceramic tile. Dab at the paint with a stencil brush and stencil the flower motif. Leave to dry completely. Apply a second coat of paint for a stronger image then remove the stencil.

3 Tape the tulip stencil upright to the centre of the upper rail of the chair. Lightly stencil the motif with the white acrylic paint. Leave to dry then remove the stencil.

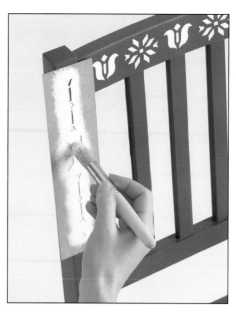

4 Stencil the tulip again at each end of the rail. Stencil a medium star flower between the tulips. If your chair does not have enough space for a medium star flower, stencil one of the smaller images instead.

5 Tape the strip stencil to one upright of the back on the chair, placing the single diamond at the centre. Shorten the stencil to fit if necessary. Stencil the upright. Leave it to dry completely then swivel the stencil, matching the single diamond position to stencil the other half of the upright.

6 Repeat this process on the other chair upright. Stencil the front and sides of the legs in the same way. Shorten the stencil or repeat the images to fit the length of your chair legs.

7 Tape the strip stencil to the lower rail, placing the small star flower at the centre. Shorten the stencil to fit if necessary. Stencil the rail.

8 Stencil the small star flower in the centre of the front seat support. Stencil any other parts of the chair using the entire strip stencil or just a section of it.

PAINTED DRAWERS

Jazz up plain drawers with bright paintbox colours and simple daisy stencils. The stencils could also be used to decorate larger pieces of furniture such as a chest of drawers for a child's room or kitchen units. Sample pots of emulsion (latex) paint are ideal to use on small projects.

You will need

- set of wooden drawers
- fine-grade abrasive paper
- emulsion (latex) paints in various bright colours
- medium and small decorator's paintbrushes
- screwdriver
- acetate sheet
- craft knife and self-healing cutting mat
- stencil brushes
- matt (flat) acrylic varnish
- wood glue (optional)

1 Remove the drawers and sand down the frame and drawers to remove any rough areas or patches of old paint.

2 Paint the drawer frame with emulsion (latex) paint. Leave to dry, then apply a second coat of paint.

3 Unscrew the drawer knobs and paint each drawer in a different-coloured emulsion paint. Leave to dry and apply a second coat. Trace the flower template at the back of the book and cut a stencil from acetate sheet using a craft knife and cutting mat.

OPPOSITE: If you use more muted colours such as pale green or cream, you can create a much subtler effect.

4 When the drawers are dry, position the flower stencil in the centre of a drawer and, using a stencil brush and paint in a contrasting colour, stencil on the flower. Leave to dry.

5 Stencil a daisy flower in the centre of each drawer, using a different colour paint for each one.

6 Paint the drawer knobs with two coats of paint, leaving them to dry between coats. Leave to dry.

7 Screw or glue a painted knob to the centre of each drawer. Varnish the drawers with matt acrylic varnish. Leave to dry before reassembling.

TRAIN TOY BOX

This chugging train stencil will fit any child's toy box. Simply add or decrease the number of wagons to suit your requirements. You could add more wagons to extend the train around the entire box.

1 Stick a length of masking tape around the toy box immediately below the intended position of the rails. Stick another length of tape 5mm/¼in above the first. Keep the tape parallel with the base of the toy box.

2 Using a flat paintbrush, spread a thin coat of grey paint on to a ceramic tile. Dab at the paint with a stencil brush and stencil the rails. Leave the paint to dry then carefully pull off the tape.

3 Trace the toy box and clouds templates at the back of the book. Tape a piece of acetate to the tracings. Using a craft knife and cutting mat cut out the stencils, cutting straight lines against a metal ruler. You will need two toy box stencils – the train engine, wagons and smoke, then the wheels and the details. Also cut out the registration marks to help guide your positioning.

4 Tape the engine, wagons and smoke stencil to the front of the box, placing the lower registration marks on the upper edge of the rails. Mark the top registration marks and the top strut of the lower registration marks with a soft pencil. Using the flat paintbrush, spread a thin coat of red paint on to the tile. Dab at the paint with a stencil brush and stencil the engine. Leave to dry.

5 Using the flat paintbrush, spread a thin coat of aquamarine and pink paint on to the tile. Stencil the wagons with the aquamarine and pink paint. Spread grey and white paint on to the tile. Dab at one paint then the other and stencil the steam to create a mottled effect. Leave to dry completely then remove the stencil.

6 Tape the wheels and details stencil in place, matching the registration marks. Stencil the chimneys using yellow paint. Stencil the wheels and couplings with blue paint. Stencil the coal with black paint. Hold the stencil brush upright when stencilling and move the brush in a circular motion. Leave to dry. Remove the stencil.

7 Move the wagon stencil along the box, matching the right-hand registration marks of the previous wagon with the left-hand registration marks of the next. Stencil the wheels and couplings with blue paint. Leave to dry. Replace the stencil with a wagon stencil, matching the registration marks. Stencil the wagon with purple paint.

8 Leave to dry then erase the registration marks. Tape the clouds stencil centrally to the lid of the box. Use the flat paintbrush to spread a thin coat of white paint on to the tile. Stencil the clouds with the white paint. Leave to dry. To make the toy box hardwearing paint it with two or three coats of clear matt (flat) varnish.

HAWAIIAN HIBISCUS CABINET

Transform a plain wooden cabinet with this flamboyant floral stencil. Enlarge the template on a photocopier to fit your cupboard door.

1 If necessary, fill any screwholes in the cabinet with wood filler. Leave to dry, then sand lightly with abrasive paper. Paint the cabinet with apricot emulsion (latex) paint. Leave to dry, then sand lightly with abrasive paper. Wipe with a damp rag. Apply a second coat of paint.

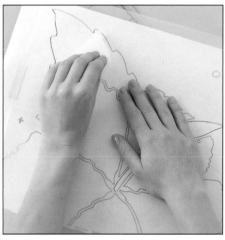

2 Enlarge the template at the back of the book on a photocopier. Tape a piece of acetate to the photocopy with masking tape. Resting on a cutting mat, cut out the stencils with a craft knife. You will need three stencils – the petals, the stigma and leaves, and the stamens and spots.

3 Stick the petals stencil to the door with spray mount. Mark the registration marks with a soft pencil. Using a flat paintbrush, spread a thin coat of pink paint on to a ceramic tile. Dab at the paint with a stencil brush and stencil the petals.

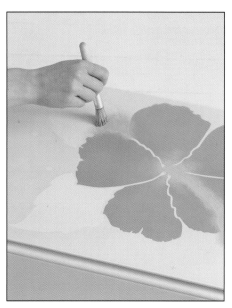

4 Leave to dry. Shade the petals at the centre of the flower with apricot acrylic paint. Leave to dry then remove the stencil.

5 Stick the stigma and leaves stencil in place with spray mount, matching the registration marks. Stencil the stigma with apricot paint.

6 Stencil the leaves with lime green paint. Leave to dry.

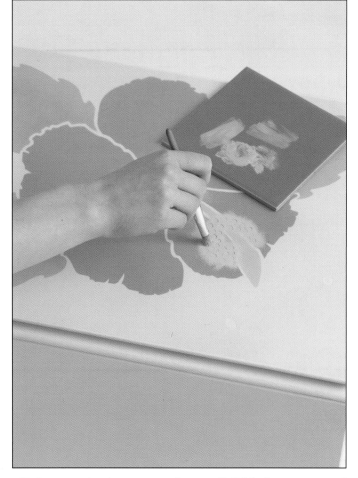

7 Shade the leaves along their centres and around the petals with mid-green paint to darken the areas and give a slight three-dimensional effect.

8 Leave to dry then remove the stencil. Stick the stamens and spots stencil to the door with spray mount, matching the registration marks. Mix a little lime green and yellow paint and use to stencil the stamens.

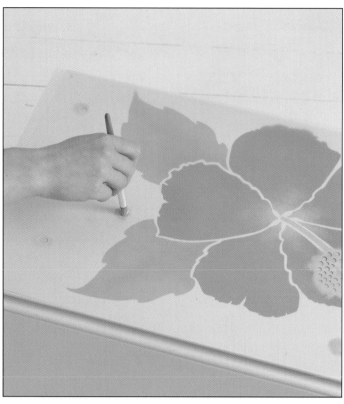

9 Stencil the spots with the mixed lime green and yellow paint. Leave to dry.

10 Shade the edges of the spots with apricot paint. Remove the stencil and erase the registration marks.

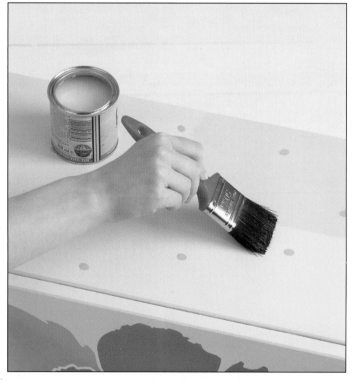

11 Position part of the spots stencil on the side of the cabinet. Tape in place and stencil the spots with the mixed lime green and yellow paint. Leave to dry. Move the stencil along to stencil another part of the side if necessary. Repeat on the other side of the cabinet and on the top if that will be visible.

12 Set the cabinet aside to dry overnight then remove the stencil. Apply two coats of clear matt varnish, lightly sanding the cabinet between coats. This will protect the cabinet from wear and tear.

OPPOSITE: Any large single flower can be used to decorate a cabinet.

CELTIC KNOT BOX

Intertwined, maze-like designs like this circular motif appeared on Irish carvings and manuscripts as early as the fifth century AD. The knot is made up of four quarters, repeated individually in the corners of the box.

You will need

- medium-grade abrasive paper
- wooden box
- wood filler (optional)
- acrylic primer
- medium decorator's paintbrush
- acrylic paints in pale and dark gold
- tracing paper and pen or carbon paper and sharp pencil
- masking tape
- stencil card
- craft knife and self-healing cutting mat
- ruler
- soft pencil
- spray mount
- stencil brush
- green stencil paint
- aerosol matt (flat) or gloss varnish

1 Sand down the box to key the surface and, if necessary, fill in any holes or deep scratches with wood filler.

2 Paint the box with a coat of white wood primer to prepare the surface. Porous wood may need two coats.

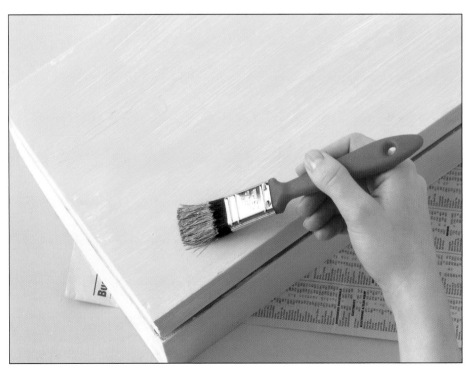

3 Paint the box with one or two layers of pale gold paint.

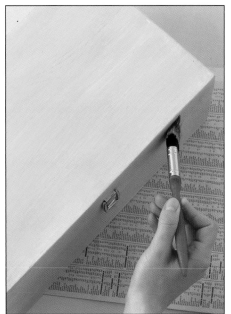

4 To give interest to the pale yellow surface of the box, colour wash it with dark gold paint. Dilute the paint with four parts of water and apply with broad strokes using a decorator's brush.

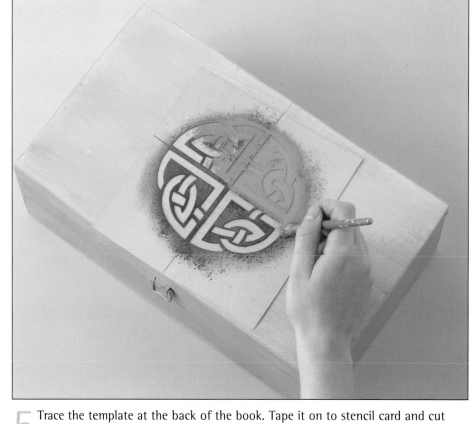

5 Trace the template at the back of the book. Tape it on to stencil card and cut out, using a craft knife and cutting mat. Mark the quarter sections on the stencil. Using a soft pencil, lightly pencil in two lines to divide the box top into quarters. Spray the stencil with spray mount, then line it up along the pencil lines and fill in with green paint.

6 Stencil in a quarter section of the knot in each corner of the box. Line it up so that the centre division of the stencil lies at the edge of the lid and mask off carefully with tape.

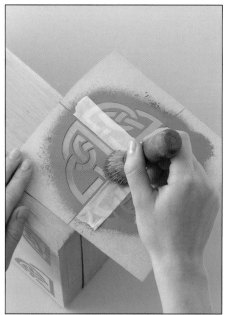

7 Stencil the bottom of each side of the box in the same way using sections of the main motif that will fit neatly into the right-angled corners. Mask off the surrounding area as necessary.

8 Once the paint is quite dry, sand the box lightly to give it a distressed finish. Spray with one or more coats of craft varnish to protect the surface with a matt (flat) or gloss finish.

DAISY STOOL

Give a simple wooden stool a new lease of life with pretty folk art motifs. The fine stripes around the legs are achieved by stencilling between strips of masking tape.

You will need

- wooden stool, painted pale green
- tracing paper and pen
- 12mm/¹⁄₂in wide masking tape
- acetate sheet
- craft knife and self-healing cutting mat
- soft pencil
- flat paintbrush
- acrylic paints in beige and dark green
- ceramic tile
- stencil brush
- piece of card (stock)
- eraser
- clear matt (flat) varnish and brush

1 Trace the templates at the back of the book. Tape a piece of acetate to the tracings. Using a craft knife and cutting mat, cut out the stencils. You will need two stencils for each seat flower – the circle and leaves, then the flower centre, petals, stalk and leaf veins. Remember to cut out the registration marks.

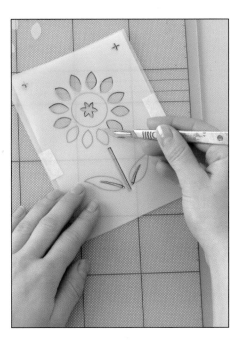

2 Measure the seat and divide it into quarters with a soft pencil. Tape the circle and leaves stencils of the seat flowers inside two of the quarters. Mark the registration marks in pencil. Using a flat paintbrush, spread a thin coat of beige paint on to a ceramic tile. Lightly dab at the paint with a stencil brush and stencil the circles and leaves holding the stencil brush upright and moving it in a circular motion. Leave to dry then repeat in the other quarters.

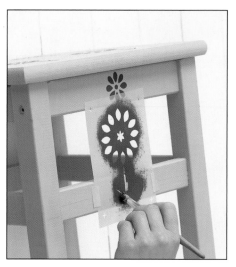

3 When the paint is dry tape the flower centre, petals, stalk and leaf veins stencils in place, matching the registration marks. Stencil the cut-outs with dark green paint. Leave to dry then repeat on the other flowers. Leave to dry then erase the pencil marks.

4 Position the small flower stencil centrally on a top strut of the stool. Carefully stencil the flower with dark green paint, protecting the surrounding area from paint with a piece of card (stock). Repeat the stencil centrally on the other top struts.

5 Tape the pair of leaves of one seat flower stencil centrally to a lower strut. Stencil the leaves with dark green paint. Leave to dry. Remove the stencil and tape the leaf veins stencil in place. Tape over the stem cut-out. Stencil the leaf veins with beige paint. Repeat on the other struts.

6 Stick three lengths of low-tack masking tape around one stool leg, leaving a 5mm/¼in gap between each tape to create stripes around the bottom of the leg.

7 Stencil the stripes with dark green paint. Repeat on the other legs. Peel off the tape when the paint has dried. Give the stool two coats of varnish to finish.

TEA TABLE

A fun approach to stencilling using a simple reverse technique that doesn't involve cutting any stencils, this trompe l'oeil table top is quick and easy to do and can transform an old table. The paper doilies give a pretty, lacy effect, complemented by the blue-and-white polka dot "tablecloth".

You will need

- medium and fine-grade abrasive paper
- electric sanding machine (optional)
- small wooden table
- medium decorator's paintbrush
- white wood primer
- spray mount
- four round paper doilies
- light blue acrylic paint
- large stencil brush
- packet of 1cm/½in adhesive dots
- piece of paper
- craft knife
- matt (flat) varnish and brush

1 Sand down the table top, sides and legs to key the surface ready for the new paint. Use medium then fine-grade abrasive paper to give a smooth finish. If you have an electric sanding machine, this will speed up the preparation.

2 Paint the table top with a coat of white primer and leave to dry completely. If you prefer a more subtle paint finish with some of the underlying colour showing through, make this a very light coat.

3 Spray the wrong side of the first doily lightly with spray mount and position it along the centre of one side of the table. Smooth it down gently with the flat of your hand, then fix the other three doilies in place spacing them at regular intervals.

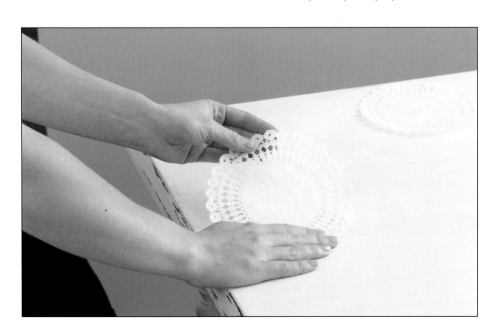

OPPOSITE: You can vary the pattern of the stencilled doilies to create an individual place setting if you wish.

4 Using a very small amount of blue paint and a dry stencil brush, block in a circle of colour around the doilies, filling in all the spaces and covering the edge completely.

5 When the paint is dry, carefully pull back and discard the doilies. Stencil the other three "mats" in the same way taking care not to overload the brush with paint.

6 Stick the adhesive dots randomly over the remaining white paint, spacing them at roughly equal intervals across the surface of the table top.

7 Using a stippling action and a dry stencil brush, paint over the rest of the table, filling in the space between the stencils with an even layer of colour.

8 Leave to dry completely. Gently lift off each adhesive dot in turn using the sharp point of a craft knife, being careful not to dig it into the wood so you do not scratch the surface of the paint.

9 Paint the rest of the table with blue paint, paying attention to any moulded areas around the top edge and on the legs. When dry, apply two coats of matt (flat) varnish to make the table top hardwearing.

AFRICAN BEDSIDE CHEST

Warm rustic colours and a bold graphic design have transformed a dull modern chest of drawers. The African motifs are stencilled across a band of subtle colour, which is applied with a natural sponge.

1 Moisten the sponge. Using a flat paintbrush, spread a thin coat of yellow ochre paint on to a ceramic tile. Dab at the paint with the sponge.

2 Dab the paint in a 12cm/4$^{1}/_{2}$in wide band on the top of the chest approximately 4cm/1$^{1}/_{2}$in from the front and back edges. Leave to dry.

3 Trace the templates at the back of the book enlarging or reducing them as necessary using a photocopier. Tape a piece of acetate to the tracings. Using a craft knife and self-healing cutting mat, cut out the stencils. Cut the straight lines freehand for a natural effect.

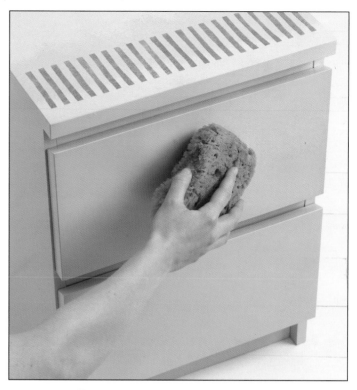

4 Stick the top stencil to the top of the chest at the front with spray mount. Using the flat paintbrush, spread a thin coat of terracotta paint on to the tile. Dab at the paint with a stencil brush and stencil the top of the chest. Move the stencil to the back of the top of the chest and repeat.

5 Using a flat paintbrush, spread a thin coat of yellow ochre acrylic paint on to the ceramic tile. Dab at the paint with a natural sponge. Dab the paint across a drawer front. Leave to dry completely.

6 Stick the zigzag stencil to one half of a drawer front with spray mount. Stencil the zigzags with terracotta paint. Leave to dry then remove the stencil.

7 Stick the rotating lines stencil to the other half of the drawer front with spray mount and stencil with terracotta paint. Leave to dry then remove the stencil. Paint with two or three coats of matt (flat) varnish to protect the chest.

STRIPED TABLE AND CHAIRS

Pencils, paintbrushes and colourful stripes will provide inspiration for the young artist in your family on this charming set of child-sized furniture.

1 Using masking tape, mask off a 30 x 20cm/12 x 8in rectangle on the centre of the table. Make sure that all the corners are right angles using a set square (triangle) and adjust the tapes if necessary.

2 Apply lengths of masking tape in rows across the rectangle to make stripes of various widths. Cut some lengths 5mm/¼in wide. To do this, stick the tape to a cutting mat and use a craft knife to cut the tape lengthwise in half, cutting against a metal ruler. Peel the tapes off the mat.

3 Using a flat paintbrush, spread the pale blue, apricot, aquamarine and lilac paints on to a ceramic tile. Dab at the paint with a stencil brush and stencil the stripes in different colours. To stop the paint straying over the 6mm/¼in wide tape, hold a piece of card over the next stripes. Leave the paint to dry then carefully pull off the tapes.

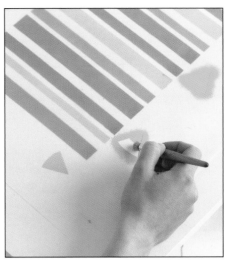

4 Trace the pencil templates at the back of the book. Tape a piece of stencil card to the tracings. Using the craft knife and cutting mat cut out the stencils, cutting straight lines against a metal ruler. You will need two pencil stencils – the wood, then the pencil and lead. You will need two paintbrush stencils – the handle and bristles, then the metal band and paint.

5 Lay the pencil stencils together on the table, matching the registration marks along two adjacent sides of the stripes. Tape the pencil wood stencil in place. Mark the registration marks with a soft pencil. Using a flat paintbrush, spread apricot paint on to a ceramic tile. Dab at the paint with a stencil brush. Stencil the pencil woods with apricot paint. Leave to dry.

6 Move the stencil to the other sides of the stripes, matching up the registration marks. Stencil the pencil woods with apricot acrylic paint as before. Leave to dry completely then remove the stencil.

7 With masking tape, secure the pencil and lead stencil to the table, matching up the registration marks exactly. Stencil the pencils and leads using lilac, aquamarine and pale blue acrylic paint. Protect the next pencil from any stray paint with a piece of card when stencilling the leads and ends of the pencils. Leave it to dry completely then move the stencil to the other side of the stripes and continue working.

8 Apply masking tape in rows across the chair seat, making some of the lengths of tape 5mm/¼in wide as before. Mask off the bottom of the chair back and around the edges of the seat.

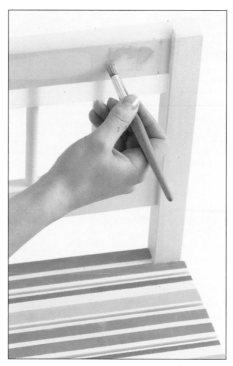

9 Stencil the seat in coloured stripes to match the table using blue, purple, apricot and an aquamarine paint. Leave the paint to dry completely then peel off the tapes.

10 Tape the paint-brush handle and bristles stencil to the top rail of the chair. Mark the registration marks. Stencil the bristles using apricot paint and stencil the handle.

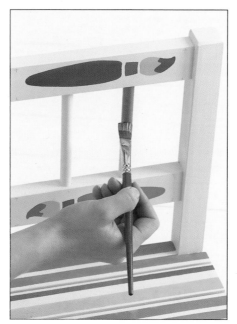

11 Tape the band and paint stencil to the top rail, matching the registration marks. Stencil the band with grey paint. Stencil the paint in a different colour. Repeat on the other rail but turn the stencil so the paintbrush is pointing in the other direction and then use different colours for the handle and paint.

12 Paint any rungs on the chair to co-ordinate with the stripes. Leave to dry then erase the registration marks. Apply two coats of clear varnish, sanding the furniture and wiping it with a damp rag between coats. This will help protect the table and chairs from wear and tear.

FLOWER POWER CHAIR

Recalling the bright floral patterns of the sixties, this colourful chair will cheer up any kitchen, bedroom or bathroom. Only the seat is decorated, giving the impression that it is covered in a vintage patterned fabric.

You will need

- medium and fine-grade abrasive paper
- wooden chair with completely flat seat
- white wood primer
- medium decorator's paintbrush
- tracing paper and pen or carbon paper and sharp pencil
- masking tape
- stencil card
- craft knife and self-healing cutting mat
- acrylic paints in blue, pink, yellow and green
- stencil brush
- clear matt (flat) varnish and brush
- white wood paint

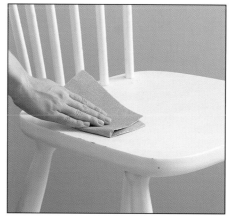

1 Sand down the chair seat with medium then fine-grade abrasive paper to prepare the surface for painting, paying special attention to any chips or scratches. Sand the legs, struts and back of the chair in the same way. You may need to repair any deep holes with wood filler.

2 Paint the whole chair with white primer. Leave to dry. Trace the templates at the back of the book and tape them on to stencil card. Cut out, using a craft knife and cutting mat. Trim the edges, leaving a small margin around the motifs, so that the stencil can be positioned close to the struts.

3 Stencil the first flower in blue, using a blocking technique and a fine dry brush. Stencil a sprinkling of blue flowers across the seat, spacing them regularly and altering the angle of each one. Make sure that you have enough space between them to fit in the pink flowers and the tiny green flowers. If you wish, you can mark the positions in with pencil before you start stencilling, to be sure that the spacing is correct.

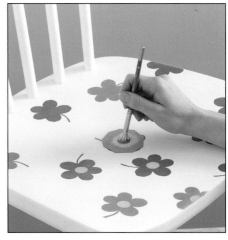

4 Fill in some of the spaces either side of the blue stencilled flowers with pink acrylic paint, using the same stencil cut out.

5 Using the same paint colours, stencil a few part flowers to overlap the edges of the seat.

6 Add yellow dots in the centre of the large flowers with the small round stencil, dabbing the brush lightly to give a slight texture.

7 Using the small flower stencil, add a few small green flowers in the remaining spaces. Leave to dry completely then protect the seat with two or three coats of matt (flat) varnish. Paint the back and legs of the chair with white wood paint. If your chair has a large flat area across the top edge or wide struts, you could add more flowers to the back. Stencilling and painting four or six different chairs in this way would give you an attractive mismatching set for a modern kitchen or dining room.

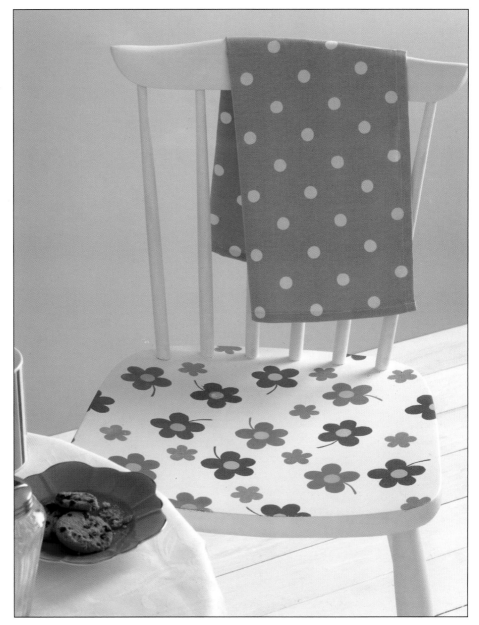

RIGHT: *Enliven an old kitchen chair by using bright, fresh colours and motifs.*

FABRICS

Stencilling is one of the oldest methods of textile printing (it was used in Japan over a thousand years ago) and the only technique for transferring patterns that can easily be done at home. Use it to decorate fabrics from sheer organza to plush velvet, with repeating, scattered or all-over designs, and then make your unique materials up into one-off soft furnishings: cushions, blinds, curtains, tablecloths and floorcloths.

ABOVE: A simple seashell motif is perfect for a summer beach bag.

*LEFT: Graphic rose print cushions add elegance to a light,
modern living room or conservatory.*

ORGANZA CUSHION

If you always thought stencilling had a simple country look, then think again. This beautiful organza cushion with gold stencilling takes the craft into the luxury class. Use the sharpest dressmaking pins when handling organza to avoid marking the fabric.

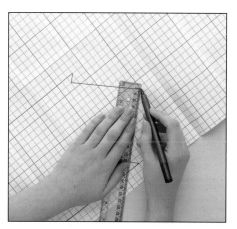

1 Copy the border template at the back of the book on to dressmaker's graph paper and cut out. In addition, cut out a 52cm/21in square and a 52 x 40cm/21 x 16in rectangle from graph paper.

2 Pin the square and rectangle to the main colour organza. Cut two 52cm/21in squares, and two rectangles measuring 52 x 40cm/21 x 16in from the main fabric. Cut four border pieces from the contrasting fabric.

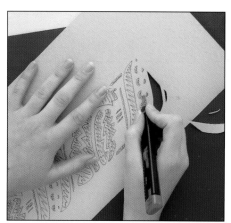

3 Cut a piece of stencil card 18 x 52cm/7 x 21in. Trace the template and transfer to the card, 8cm/3¼in from the bottom edge and with 6cm/2½in to spare at each end. Cut out the stencil using a craft knife and a self-healing cutting mat.

4 Spray the back of the stencil with spray mount and position along the edge of the main organza fabric square. Cut two 45-degree mitres from stencil card, spray with adhesive and press in place. Mask off the surrounding areas with paper.

5 Spray with gold paint. Leave to
dry and spray again. Remove
the masking paper and stencil. Place the
stencil along the next edge, put the
mitres in place and continue as before.
Stencil the remaining two sides. Hem one
long edge of each fabric rectangle by
folding over 1cm/$^1/_2$in, then 1.5cm/$^5/_8$in.
Pin, tack (baste) and machine stitch the
hem, then press.

6 Lay the stencilled fabric square face
down and the second square on top.
Lay the two rectangles on top of these
squares, overlapping the stitched edges
so that the raw edges line up with the
square pieces. Pin, tack and machine
stitch 1cm/$^1/_2$in from the raw edge.
Trim the seam allowance to 5mm/$^1/_4$in.
Then, pin, tack and stitch the border
pieces together at the mitred corners
1cm/$^1/_2$in from the raw edges. Trim the
corners and turn the material the right
way out. Press the fabric with a
protective cloth. Continue until the
border pieces make a ring.

7 Using a protective cloth, press
one of the raw edges under by
1cm/$^1/_2$in. Lay the pressed edge of
the border fabric along the edge of the
main fabric square and pin, tack and
stitch in place.

8 Turn the cushion over and pull the
border over. Turn under the border's
raw edge by 1cm/$^1/_2$in and pin in place
along the front of the cushion. Them
tack and stitch in place. Press and insert
the cushion pad.

FIFTIES ROSE CUSHIONS

Reminiscent of the stylized designs of the 1950s, these rose print cushions would look at home in a classic or contemporary setting. Use your imagination to create more variations on the theme and alter the number of roses on each cushion.

1 Wash the fabric to remove any dressing and press to remove any creases before cutting out the panels. Place the first panel on a pad of newspaper to absorb paint, then check the position of the stencil by placing it over the square.

2 Cut out the stalk and four flower head stencils from acetate using a heat knife or an ordinary craft knife. Spray the reverse of the large rose background stencil with spray mount, then position it towards the top left corner. Block it in with coral paint, using a dry stencil brush.

3 Leave the paint to dry completely, then line up the large petal stencil over the background. Fill it in with a small amount of aubergine paint to complete the rose.

4 Spray the back of the stalk stencil and place it diagonally across the fabric. Fill it in with dark green fabric paint, again loading the brush with the minimum amount to prevent seepage.

5 The design on the second cushion cover consists of one large and two small roses. Stencil in the rose backgrounds first using coral paint, positioning them so that they point towards the centre of the cushion.

6 Using aubergine paint, add the second layer (the petal stencil) to each of the roses. Line the stencils up by eye so that they fit within the area already painted, and secure in place with spray mount.

7 Stencil in the stalks, allowing the lower part of each one to overlap the edge of the fabric. Leave to dry, then iron both covers on the back to fix (set) the paint, following the instructions supplied by the manufacturer.

8 To make up each cushion cover, stitch a narrow seam along one long edge of the two back panels. With right sides facing and the three raw edges lined up, place one at each side of the front panel so that the seams overlap. Pin and tack (baste) in place, then machine stitch 1cm/¹/₂in from the outside edge. Clip the surplus fabric from the corners and ease the corners into shape with the point of a pencil. Turn through and press using a cloth to protect the stencilled side of the cover, then insert the square cushion pad through the opening.

RIGHT: Vary the number of roses on each of the cushions to make them different.

DRAGONFLY CURTAIN

Beautiful, fragile dragonflies hover on this delicate muslin (cheesecloth) curtain. The wing tips of the dragonflies are shaded in a contrasting colour and the insects are stencilled singly and in groups of three.

You will need

- tracing paper and pen
- masking tape
- acetate
- craft knife and self-healing cutting mat
- sheer curtain
- iron
- plastic carrier bag
- ceramic tile
- flat paintbrush
- stencil brush
- fabric paints in lilac and aquamarine

1 Trace the template at the back of the book. Attach a piece of acetate to the tracing with masking tape. Cut out the stencil using a craft knife and self-healing cutting mat, cutting carefully around the acute curved edges.

2 Iron the curtain to remove creases. Lay a section of the curtain out flat on a plastic carrier bag, to protect the work surface. Tape the stencil smoothly to the fabric with masking tape. Stencil the dragonfly with lilac fabric paint. Leave to dry.

3 Stencil the tips of the dragonfly wings with aquamarine paint. Leave to dry then remove the stencil.

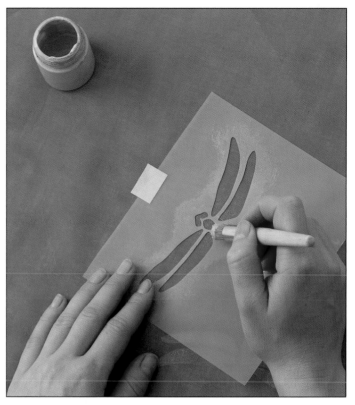

4 Move the stencil to the next position, close to the first dragonfly but not touching it. Tape it in place and stencil as before.

5 When the paint is dry, move the stencil again so that the dragonflies are positioned to "hover" in a group of three. Stencil the third dragonfly.

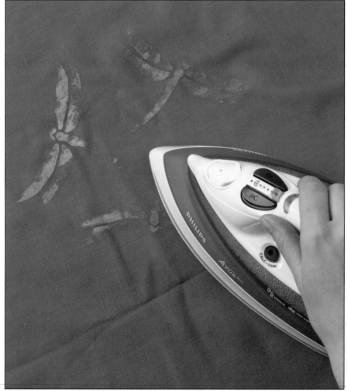

6 Move the stencil and place it at random on the curtain. Stencil a single dragonfly. Continue stencilling dragonflies all over the curtain in groups of three and singly.

7 Leave the paint to dry overnight then iron the curtain on the wrong side to fix (set) the paint, following the manufacturer's instructions.

RAINFOREST CURTAINS

Both the positive and negative parts of this stencil are used to create a sophisticated pattern from a single, almost abstract motif. Light streaming through the unlined cotton enhances the hothouse look of this design.

You will need

- scissors
- lightweight plain cotton fabric, to fit window
- tape measure
- iron
- dressmaking pins
- sewing machine
- matching thread
- needle
- buttons
- acetate sheet
- masking tape
- craft knife and self-healing cutting mat
- tailor's chalk
- newspaper
- spray mount
- green fabric paint
- large stencil brush

1 Cut the cotton fabric to required size for the curtains, allowing 5cm/2in seam allowances at the sides and lower edge and 2cm/¾in at the top. Press under, pin and machine-stitch 2.5cm/1in double hems down each side, then repeat the process for the hem at the bottom of the curtain.

2 Calculate the number of tabs you will need, spacing them about 20cm/8in apart. Cut a rectangle of fabric for each tab, using the template at the back of the book. Fold each rectangle in half lengthways and stitch, with a 1cm/½in seam allowance. Open out the seam allowance and pin and stitch across one end of the tab so that the seam lies at the centre.

3 Turn each tab to the right side and press. Pin the raw ends of the material to the right side of each curtain, spacing the tabs evenly along the top. For the facing, cut a 7.5cm/3in strip of fabric the width of the curtain plus 4cm/1½in for seam allowances. Pin the strip to the curtain with right sides together and then machine-stitch the top edge.

4 Fold the facing to the wrong side, fold in the seam allowances at each end and along the raw edge and then pin in place.

5 Machine-stitch the facing close to the folded edge.

6 Fold the tabs over on to the front side of the curtain and then hand-stitch one of the buttons to hold each tab in place.

7 Enlarge the stencil template at the back of the book on a photocopier to your desired size. Cut a square of acetate sheet the size of the design and fasten it to the design with tabs of masking tape. Cut out using a craft knife and cutting mat. Retain the cut-out part of the stencil for the negative images.

8 Using tailor's chalk, mark the curtains into squares the same size as the stencil. Protect the work surface. Using spray mount, attach the stencil in place in the first marked square. Apply fabric paint with the stencil brush to create a mottled effect. Leave the stencil in place. To make the negative image, mask off the areas around the square with tape.

9 Use spray mount to fix the cut-out motif in the centre, then apply green fabric paint all around it. Remove the stencil and move it to the next marked square. Repeat this pattern all over the curtain. Leave to dry completely then iron the curtain on the wrong side to fix (set) the paint following the manufacturer's instructions.

SPRIGGED CURTAIN

This repeating pattern is easy to achieve if you iron the curtain fabric to mark a grid before you start to stencil. Alternatively, the leaf motif could be stencilled randomly across the fabric for a more informal look. Wash and iron the fabric before you start.

You will need

- tracing paper and pen
- stencil card
- craft knife and self-healing cutting mat
- cotton voile to fit window
- iron
- newspaper
- masking tape
- spray mount
- fabric paints in green, blue, brown and pink
- stencil brushes
- sewing machine
- matching sewing thread
- curtain wire

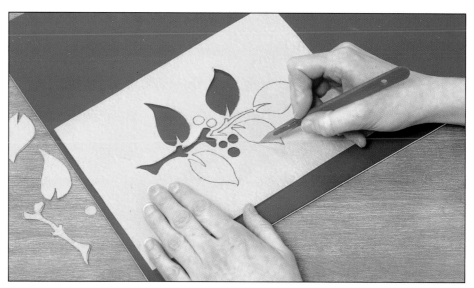

1 Enlarge the template at the back of the book on a photocopier so that it is 17cm/6½in high. Transfer the outline to stencil card and cut out using a craft knife and cutting mat. Fold the fabric into 20cm/8in vertical pleats and 25cm/10in horizontal pleats, then iron lightly to leave a grid pattern. Cover the work surface with newspaper and tape the fabric down so that it is fairly taut.

2 Spray the back of the stencil with spray mount and place it in the first rectangle. Mix (combine) the fabric paints to achieve subtle shades. Stencil the leaves in green, adding blue at the edges for depth. Stencil the stem in brown and the berries in a brownish pink. Repeat in alternate rectangles.

3 Turn the stencil upside down and, using pink fabric paint, stencil the top leaf in the centre of the plain rectangles. Add a darker shade at the tip and mark the stalk in brown. Iron the curtain on the wrong side to fix (set) the paints according to the manufacturer's instructions. Hem the sides and lower edge of the curtain. Make a 2.5cm/1in channel at the top and then insert the curtain wire.

BELOW: Use soft shades of green and pink to create a light, elegant look to this small curtain.

ZODIAC CAFÉ CURTAIN

Use gold fabric paints to dramatize a plain muslin (cheesecloth) curtain. Paint the shapes at random on the curtain, but try to plan your design so that they all appear frequently. Add variety by blending the two shades of gold on some of the designs.

You will need

- tracing paper and pen
- stencil card
- craft knife and self-healing cutting mat
- kitchen paper
- newspaper
- white muslin (cheesecloth), to fit window
- iron
- masking tape
- spray mount
- fabric paints in light and dark gold
- stencil brushes
- sewing machine
- matching thread
- curtain clips and metal rings

1 Trace the stencil motifs from the back of the book. Transfer on to 12 rectangles of stencil card and cut out using a craft knife and cutting mat. Practise your stencilling technique on some spare fabric. Don't overload your brush and wipe off any excess paint on kitchen paper before you begin.

2 Cover your work table with newspaper. Iron the muslin, then tape one corner to the table with masking tape, keeping it flat. Coat the back of each stencil lightly with spray mount before positioning it on the fabric. Stencil with the light gold fabric paint, then stencil over the edges of the motif with dark gold to give depth. Leave to dry, then gently peel the stencil off.

3 Cover the rest of the fabric with the zodiac motifs, repositioning it on the work table as necessary and stencilling one section at a time. Leave to dry then iron the curtain on the wrong side to fix (set) the paints according to the manufacturer's instructions. Hem the edges and attach the curtain clips to the upper edge of the material.

BELOW: You can change the colours of the zodiac symbols to suit your existing colour scheme if you wish.

CITRUS ROLLER BLIND

The stylized, almost abstract, oranges and lemons on this stencilled blind (shade) give it a fifties feel. It would look great in a kitchen decorated with strong, fresh colours.

You will need

- tracing paper and pen
- stencil card
- craft knife and self-healing cutting mat
- plain white cotton fabric, to fit window
- newspaper
- masking tape
- acrylic gouache paints in orange, yellow, lime green, black and red
- stencil brushes
- fabric stiffener spray
- large decorator's paintbrush
- roller blind (shade) kit

1 Enlarge the template at the back of the book on a photocopier so that the repeat design will fit across the width of your blind (shade) and trace it. Transfer it three times on to stencil card. Using a craft knife and cutting mat, cut out only the areas you will need for each stencil: (1) the lemons, oranges and red spots; (2) the leaves; (3) the black details.

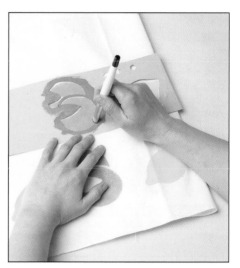

2 Lay out the white cotton fabric on the work surface, covered with newspaper, and secure with masking tape. Using gouache paints, carefully stencil the oranges and lemons motif all over the fabric. Keep the stencil brush as dry as possible, blotting off excess paint, and clean the stencil if paint starts to bleed under the edges.

3 Leave the orange and lemon motifs to dry, then proceed with the remaining colours. Stencil the leaves next, then the red spots (using the first stencil) and finally the black details. Leave to dry then spray the fabric with fabric stiffener following the manufacturer's instructions and hang on a washing line to dry, keeping it straight. Make up the blind using the blind kit.

GARDEN SHADOWS BLIND

Recreate a bright summer's day in the garden on the gloomiest of dull winter mornings with the beautiful patterns formed as shafts of sunlight cast shadows from clematis and jasmine climbing plants on to a white wall.

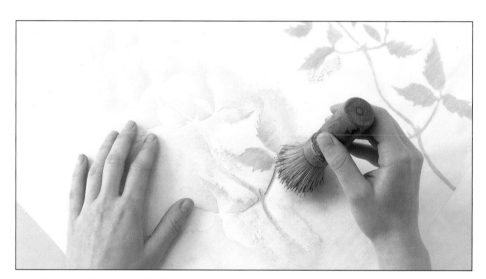

1 Wash and iron the fabric then place it on a pad of newspaper. Cut out the templates at the back of the book from acetate. Starting at the top centre edge, fix the clematis stencil in place with a light spray of adhesive. Stencil it in with silver fabric paint.

2 Moving down the fabric, stencil a second spray of clematis so that it appears to be joined on to the first. Add another long clematis spray in the same way, just to one side. Use only a small amount of paint at a time to prevent seepage, and build up two or three thin layers of paint to give solid colour.

3 Stencil in a spray of jasmine on the other side, starting it again at the top edge. This will give a denser look to the top part of the design, with the other tendrils trailing down from a leafy branch.

4 Continue stencilling until the fabric is covered, keeping the bottom part less densely patterned with just a few stems trailing down towards the edge.

5 Leave the fabric to dry completely. Fix (set) the paint according to the manufacturer's instructions using a hot iron and coat it with fabric stiffener, again following the manufacturer's instructions supplied.

6 Check the width of the finished blind (shade) once again against the actual window space, then trim the two side edges to this measurement. Mark in the cutting lines with a set square and ruler so that they are straight.

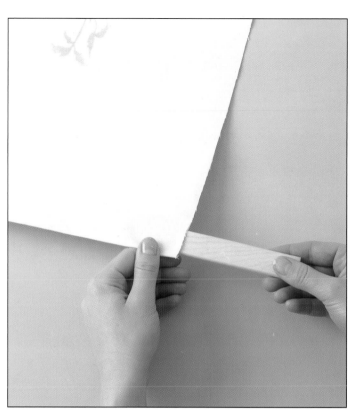

7 Using a hacksaw, cut the wooden batten (furring strip) so that it is 1cm/½in shorter than the finished width of the blind. Sand the ends to neaten, if necessary.

8 Following the directions given with the blind kit, press and stitch a channel along the lower edge. Insert the batten into the channel.

9 Cut the wooden roller to size and attach the metal fittings as directed. Fix the top edge of the blind to the adhesive tape supplied on the roller. Add the tacks if necessary to secure it in place.

10 Knot the acorn on to the cord, then thread the other end through the oval metal plate as shown in the instructions. Screw it in place at the centre back of the batten, then fix the blind to the window.

MOSAIC TABLECLOTH

Create a mosaic-effect border with a Moroccan flavour for a kitchen tablecloth using one simple stencil and a subtle blue and aqua colour combination. Hem with smart mitred corners, or simply press the edges of the tablecloth with an iron and stitch them with a sewing machine.

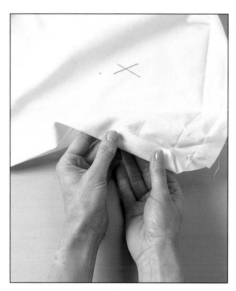

1 Press under a 2.5cm/1in wide double hem along all four edges of the cotton fabric square. Open out the fold at each corner and cut diagonally across with scissors to reduce the bulk at the corners.

2 At each corner in turn, refold the complete hem on one edge. Fold the corner of the other edge of the fabric in at right angles to meet the inside crease.

3 Refold the hem to form a neat mitred edge.

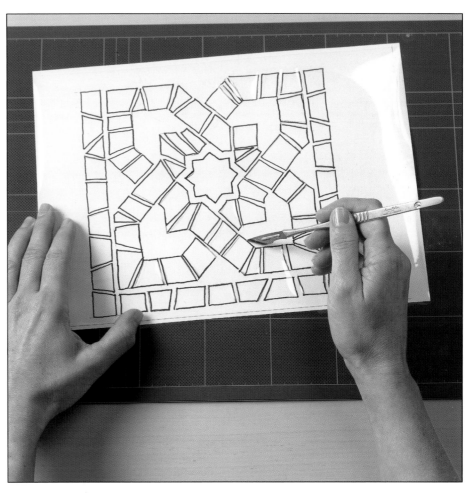

4 Pin the mitred corner into place and then repeat with the other three corners. Stitch the hem close to the inside folded edge.

5 Trace the template at the back of the book. Attach it to a piece of acetate sheet with masking tape. Carefully cut out the stencil using a craft knife and self-healing cutting mat.

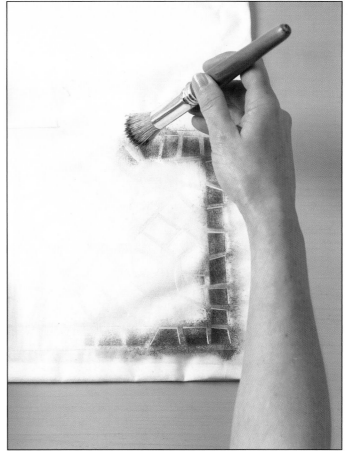

6 Cover the work surface with newspaper. Place the stencil in position on the edge of the tablecloth and secure with small strips of masking tape.

7 Using a stencil brush, take up a small amount of dark blue fabric paint and carefully apply to the outer border of the stencil, dabbing lightly.

8 Apply light blue paint to the inner sections, leaving the central motif clear.

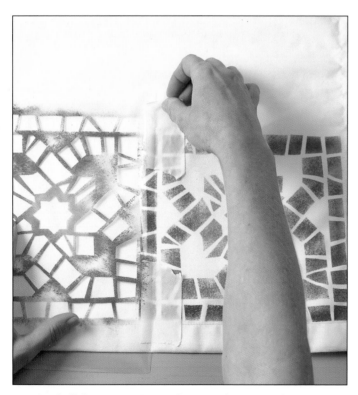

9 Apply light aqua paint to the central star motif. Remove the stencil and place it in the next position along the edge of the tablecloth. Repeat this pattern until the mosaic border is complete. Stencil the central star motif randomly over the centre of the tablecloth. Leave to dry then iron on the wrong side to fix (set) the paints, following the manufacturer's instructions.

ROSE TABLECLOTH

Two stencils are arranged here to decorate a square tablecloth; the same motifs could be used in many different combinations and sizes. Use two or three shades with each stencil shape to give a rounded, three-dimensional look to the roses, leaves and branches.

You will need

- tracing paper and pen
- stencil card or acetate
- craft knife and self-healing cutting mat
- 76cm/30in square of heavy white cotton fabric
- iron
- newspaper
- spray mount
- fabric paints in dark pink, pale pink, yellow, dark green, light green and warm brown
- stencil brushes
- vanishing fabric marker
- long ruler and T-square
- sewing machine
- white sewing thread

1 Enlarge the rose template at the back of the book on a photocopier so that it measures 15cm/6in across. Enlarge the branch template so that it is 30cm/12in long. Transfer both on to stencil card or acetate and carefully cut out using a craft knife and self-healing cutting mat.

2 Cover the work surface with newspaper. Fold the fabric in half each way, to find the centre. Press lightly along the creases. Spray the back of the rose stencil with spray mount and place it in the middle of the cloth. Stencil the rose, starting with dark pink paint in the corner petals and around the outer edge of the inner petals.

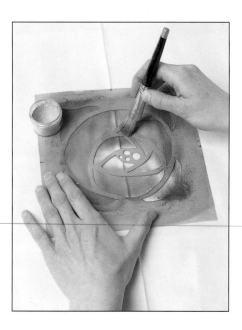

3 Fill in the rest of the petals with pale pink and colour the centre dots in yellow. Keep the brush upright and use a small circling motion to transfer the paint. Be careful not to overload the bristles. Peel off the stencil and allow the paint to dry.

4 Work a branch motif on each side of the rose, using the crease as a placement guide, to form a cross. Spray the back of the card with adhesive, as before. Stencil yellow paint in the centre of each leaf.

5 Blend dark and light green paint and finish painting the leaves.

6 Work a small amount of brown fabric paint around the base of the leaves and the outside edge of the branches. Stencil a rose at the end of each branch. With a vanishing fabric marker, and using the ruler and T-square to get a perfectly accurate square, draw a line about 15cm/6in from each edge so that it is on the same level as the outer edge of the roses. Stencil a rose in each corner and then work a branch between the roses.

7 Leave the paint to dry then iron the tablecloth on the wrong side to fix (set) according to the manufacturer's instructions. To finish the tablecloth, turn under, press and stitch a narrow double hem along the outside edge.

BELOW: *If your tablecloth is larger than 76cm/30in, add in more rows of this stencilled rose pattern to fit the size of your chosen cloth.*

SUMMER QUILT COVER

A combination of stencilling and sponging is used to decorate this ready-made duvet cover. Choose light colours for the stripes so that the stencilling will show up.

1 Cover the work surface with newspaper. Protect the back of the duvet cover from paint bleeding through by unpicking the sides of the cover and opening it out into a large rectangle. Roll up the underside of the cover and pin it so that it is out of the way. Lay out the upper side of the duvet with the area to be painted ironed flat.

2 Enlarge the templates at the back of the book on a photocopier, to suit your design. Trace on to stencil card and cut out using a craft knife and a self-healing cutting mat.

3 Using tailor's chalk, mark stripes across the duvet. First mark the position of the stripes at the edge of the duvet, making them deep enough for the stencils to fit. Then mark the midpoint on each stripe. Using a piece of string stretched across the duvet and pinned at each side, rule these lines across.

4 Dilute the fabric paint with water to the consistency of ink. Using the large household sponge, fill in the stripes of colour. Do not worry if the edges are a little rough, because this will make the final effect look more interesting. Leave each section of paint to dry before moving on to the next.

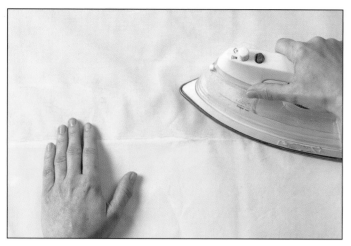

5 When the whole area is painted and completely dry, iron the fabric on the reverse to fix (set) the paint according to the manufacturer's instructions.

6 Spray the reverse of a stencil with spray mount. Place it on the midpoint of a stripe and apply colours using a small sponge or stencil brush.

7 Continue to stencil, keeping the motifs evenly spaced. After removing each stencil from the fabric, wipe away the excess paint to keep the colours clean.

8 Try blending colours together to give the finished stencil a textured appearance.

9 When the stencilling has been completed and the paint is thoroughly dry, iron again on the wrong side to fix (set) the paints according to the manufacturer's instructions.

10 Pin and stitch the side seams of the duvet cover. The fabric may seem stiff at first but washing it should solve this.

FEATHER THROW

The fringed border of this beautiful throw is created by simply pulling away the woven threads along each edge. Choose a fabric with a square, rather than a twill, weave that can easily be unravelled. Linen or heavy cotton would be ideal.

You will need

- iron
- approximately 1.3m/50in square of cream furnishing fabric
- tape measure
- scissors
- carbon paper and sharp pencil
- stencil card
- craft knife and self-healing cutting mat
- spray mount
- fabric paints in brown and white
- saucer
- large stencil brush
- pressing cloth

1 Wash the fabric to remove any chemical residue and press it well. Cut it into a perfect 1.3m/50in square by snipping between the threads to get a straight line along each edge.

2 To make the fringed edging, carefully unravel the fabric, one thread at a time, for a distance of 4cm/1½in along each side.

3 Enlarge the template at the back of the book on a photocopier and transfer it on to the stencil card using carbon paper. Cut it out, using a sharp craft knife and self-healing cutting mat. Spray the back lightly with spray mount and place it on the first corner. Mix a small amount of white and brown fabric paint in a saucer and stipple the feather with a dry brush.

4 Repeat the motif at roughly regular intervals across the fabric, altering the angle of the stencil so that the feathers are positioned randomly. Mix two shades of brown paint to make some of them light and others slightly darker, giving variety to the pattern.

5 Following the manufacturer's instructions, fix (set) the paint by ironing it with a hot steam iron and pressing cloth.

RIGHT: *This throw is made from an upholstery-weight fabric, which gives it a rather heavy look, ideal to go across the arm of a chair or back of a sofa. Stencilling on to organza or a metallic voile would make a much more ethereal version to drape over a romantically dressed bed or to hang at a window.*

LOVE PILLOWS

Make sure the message gets across by stencilling the word "love" on your pillows in both English and French. The typeface used is Gill Sans Bold, enlarged here to 42.5cm/17in long. Always pre-wash and iron the fabric to remove any glazes that could block the colour absorption.

You will need

- spray mount
- 2 pieces of stencil card
- craft knife and self-healing cutting mat
- sheet of thin card (stock)
- white cotton pillowcases
- red fabric paint
- plate
- stencil brush
- iron

1 Enlarge the templates at the back of the book to the required size on a photocopier. Coat the backs of the photocopies with spray mount and stick them to the stencil card.

2 Cut out the letters using a craft knife and cutting mat. The O, A and R need ties to retain the internal letter features, so draw in "bridges" before you cut out the letters.

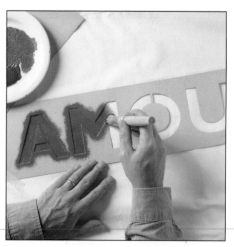

3 Place a sheet of thick card (stock) inside the pillowcase, so that the paint colour does not bleed through to the other side.

4 Stencil the letters. Leave to dry then remove the card and iron the pillow cases on the reverse side to set the paint following the manufacturer's instructions.

GIRL'S BED CANOPY AND CUSHION

This must be the ultimate design for a very feminine bedroom. The muslin (cheesecloth) canopy is stencilled with fairies and hearts and tied with heart-stencilled ribbons.

You will need

- tracing paper and pen
- masking tape
- acetate
- craft knife and self-healing cutting mat
- iron
- bright pink muslin (cheesecloth) bed canopy
- plastic bag
- ceramic tile
- flat paintbrush
- stencil brush
- fabric paints in pale pink and bright pink
- 3m/10ft of 5cm/2in wide pale pink satin ribbon
- bodkin
- dressmaker's pins
- sewing needle and pale pink sewing thread
- scissors
- 40cm/16in of 90cm/36in wide mid-pink thick cotton fabric
- 40cm/16in of 1.5m/5ft wide mid-pink chenille fabric
- sewing machine
- mid-pink sewing thread
- toy filling
- 60cm/24in pale pink marabou trim

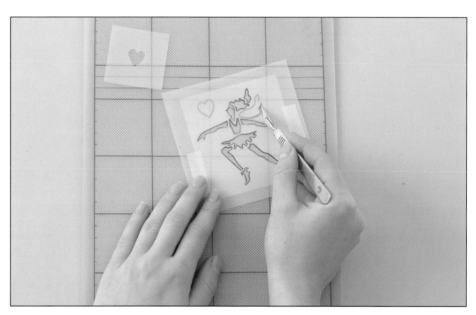

1 Trace the templates at the back of the book. Tape a piece of stencil card to the tracings. Using a craft knife and cutting mat, cut out one fairy stencil and one heart stencil.

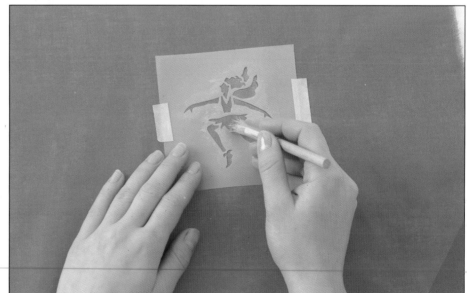

2 Iron the muslin (cheesecloth) canopy to remove creases. Lay a section out flat on a plastic bag, to stop paint seeping through to your work surface. Tape the fairy stencil to the fabric and stencil with pale pink fabric paint.

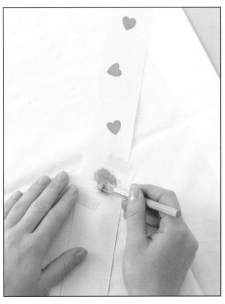

3 Move the stencil to another position on the fabric and turn it at a different angle. Tape in place and stencil the fairy again.

4 Tape the heart stencil to the canopy. Stencil the heart then continue stencilling the fairy at random all over the front and sides of the canopy, adding the heart in any gaps.

5 Cut one 1m/1yd length of ribbon for a drawstring for the top of the canopy and four 48cm/19in lengths for the ties. Stencil hearts at random on the ribbons using bright pink paint.

6 Leave the paint to dry overnight then iron the canopy and ribbons on the wrong side to fix (set) the paint, following the manufacturer's instructions. Thread the drawstring through the channel at the top of the canopy with a bodkin and adjust the ends of the drawstring to extend equally from the channel. With a hot iron, press under 1.5cm/⅝in at one end of each tie.

7 Pin and tack (baste) the pressed end of one ribbon to the canopy where it can be fastened around the opening edges. Pin and tack a corresponding ribbon underneath in the same position. Stitch close to the pressed edge then 1cm/½in from the first stitching. Repeat to attach the remaining ties. Trim all the ribbon ends diagonally.

8 Cut a 34 x 31cm/13$^{1}/_{2}$ x 12$^{1}/_{4}$in rectangle of mid-pink cotton fabric for the cushion front. With the long edges as the horizontal edges of the cushion, stencil three fairies across the centre using bright pink paint.The outer fairies should be at least 4cm/1$^{1}/_{2}$in within the short edges.

9 Stencil five hearts above and below the fairies using bright pink paint positioning the hearts at different jaunty angles. The hearts should be at least 4cm/1$^{1}/_{2}$in within the long edges. Leave to dry overnight then iron on the wrong side to fix the paint according to the manufacturer's instructions.

10 Cut two 31 x 10cm/12$^{1}/_{2}$ x 4in rectangles of chenille fabric for the borders, and a 48 x 31cm/19 x 12$^{1}/_{2}$in rectangle for the back. With right sides facing, pin the borders to the side edges of the front. Machine stitch, leaving a 1.5cm/$^{5}/_{8}$in seam allowance. Press the seams toward the borders.

 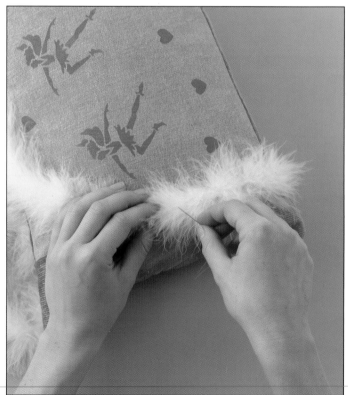

11 With right sides facing, pin the front and back together. Stitch, leaving a 1.5cm/$^{5}/_{8}$in seam allowance and a 20cm/ 8in gap to turn through. Clip the corners. Turn the cushion right side out and fill with toy filling. Slip-stitch the gap closed.

12 Stitch marabou trim along the front seams by handsewing with a double length of thread through the central core of the trim.

SEASHELL BEACH BAG

Crisp cream and navy give this smart beach bag a nautical look. Much of the charm of the stencilling lies in combining colours to give a three-dimensional look to the seashell shapes, so it's worth practising on spare fabric or lining paper first.

You will need

- iron
- 55 x 75cm/21½ x 30in cream cotton drill fabric
- scissors
- tracing paper and pen
- stencil card
- craft knife and self-healing cutting mat
- spray mount
- 2 lengths of blue cotton drill fabric or denim, each 15 x 38cm/6 x 15in
- fabric paints in dark yellow, dark red and navy blue
- stencil brushes
- sewing machine
- white, dark orange and blue sewing threads
- dressmaking pins
- 2m/6ft cream cotton cord
- masking tape

1 Wash and iron the cream fabric then cut in two lengthways. Trace the stencil from the back of the book or enlarge it on a photocopier. Transfer the outline to stencil card and cut out using a craft knife and cutting mat. Coat the back lightly with spray mount, and stencil five shells on each piece of fabric, using two or three colours. Leave to dry then iron on the reverse side to fix (set) the paint according to the manufacturer's instructions.

2 With the fabric right sides together, stitch a blue strip to the top edge of each cream piece, leaving a 1cm/½in seam allowance. Press the seam upward. Pin the rectangles right sides together, and stitch around the main bag. Press under the seam allowances on the open sides of the blue fabric, and topstitch in orange sewing thread. Fold in half lengthways. Machine-stitch parallel to the topstitch.

3 Cut the cord in half, and bind the ends with masking tape. Thread both pieces through the bag. Remove the tape, and bind the ends with blue thread, 5cm/2in from the ends. Fringe and comb the cord to make tassels. Trim neatly.

OPPOSITE: The choice of navy blue and red gives this beach bag a nautical look.

GINGERBREAD APRON

This apron wraps right around the waist so will protect clothing from the stickiest of fingers. The gingerbread pattern is so appealing there will be no question about young chefs wanting to put it on before creating their culinary masterpieces.

You will need

- cream cotton fabric, height the distance from the child's collar to the knee and width the child's waist measurement
- iron
- pencil
- scissors
- sewing needle and thread
- sewing machine
- cream thread
- tracing paper and pen or carbon paper and sharp pencil
- masking tape
- stencil card
- craft knife and self-healing cutting mat
- newspaper
- stencil brush
- fabric paints in ochre, brown, black and red
- fine artist's paintbrush
- 1m/30in of 2.5cm/1in-wide cream or white ribbon or tape

1 Wash and press the fabric. Fold it in half widthways and mark the child's waist position at the side edges. Mark a point 7.5cm/3in from the fold at the top edge and draw a curve between these two points. Cut along this curve, through both layers of fabric. Check the size against the child and alter if necessary. Neaten the cut edges with a 1cm/½in seam. Tack (baste) then machine stitch.

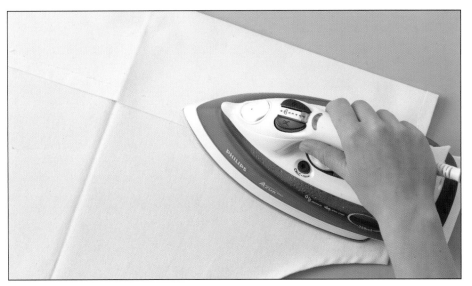

2 Fold the apron in half widthways again and press along the crease, then press a turning about 12cm/4½in from the bottom edge. These creases will act as a guide for positioning the stencil.

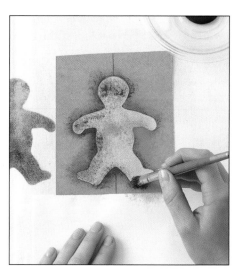

3 Trace the template at the back of the book and tape it on to stencil card. Using a craft knife and cutting mat, cut it out. Place the fabric on a layer of newspaper. Position the stencil in the centre of the apron so that the feet touch the horizontal crease. Using a dry brush, stipple it in with a light layer of ochre paint.

4 Add a stippling of brown paint around the edges of the stencil to give a more three-dimensional look to the gingerbread figure. Any irregularities in the surface will add to the cookie-like texture, so the paint does not have to be too smooth or densely applied.

5 Stencil in another two gingerbread figures at either side, varying the density of colour in each one to give them an individual appearance. Keep their feet along the crease so that they stand in a straight row. Measure the distance between their hands before positioning the stencil to make sure they are evenly spaced.

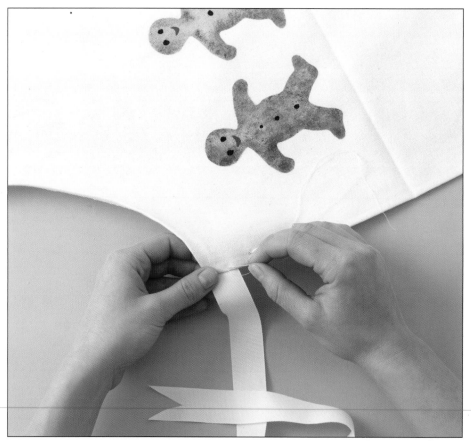

6 Using a fine artist's paintbrush, paint in two black "currant" circles for the eyes and a red semicircular "cherry slice" mouth to complete the face on the gingerbread men. Each one can have their own individual expression if you wish. Paint three "currant" buttons down their bodies. Leave to dry completely, then iron the apron on the reverse to fix (set) the paint, following the manufacturer's instructions.

7 Cut two 30cm/12in lengths of ribbon and trim one end of each into a fishtail shape. Stitch the other ends in position at the waist. Stitch the remaining ribbon in a loop at the neck.

SEVENTIES FLOWER CANVASES

Stencilling doesn't have to have a folk art theme as this set of bold canvases shows. Adapt the colours to suit your own room scheme and choose from a range of different-sized canvases, available from good art suppliers.

1 Most shop-bought canvases are already primed, but if you are reusing an old canvas or have made your own, paint all three with a layer of acrylic primer. Leave to dry completely.

2 Paint the first canvas with a base coat of turquoise paint. Trace the templates at the back of the book and tape them on to stencil card. Using a craft knife and cutting mat, cut them out. You can make the stamen stencils from either card or acetate.

3 Using orange paint, stencil a large flower on to the coloured background, with a thick brush. Apply the paint in two thin layers and use the blocking technique (see Stencilling Basics section) to give a dense colour. Make sure no acrylic primer shows through.

4 Start on the second canvas while the first one is drying. Stencil a large turquoise flower on to the top surface, applying two thin layers of paint and using the blocking technique to give a dense colour.

5 You will also need to colour in the areas where the petals overlap the edges. Hold the stencil against the side and draw in the outline with a pencil to complete the petal shape. Fill in with matching paint, using a fine brush.

6 Stencil a small white flower to overlap the orange flower on the turquoise canvas.

7 Using bright pink paint, stencil in the stamens over the centre of the large flower.

8 Add the stamens to the two flowers on the small canvas. If you wish, you can make a third painting to go with these two, using the canvas that appears at the bottom left of the finished picture as a guide to colour and layout. The variations on this theme are endless. Choose colours to match any colour scheme, arrange nine squares in three rows of three, or make just one enormous canvas for real visual impact.

OPPOSITE: Limit your choice of paint colours to three and allow the white of the artist's primer to show through.

AMISH FLOORCLOTH

Floorcloths were very popular in America during the 18th century, using painted sailcloth canvas to imitate chequered marble floors or the geometric designs of oriental carpets. The pattern for this floorcloth is adapted from an Amish quilt and the colours are also Amish-inspired, but you can use any combination.

You will need

- 1.5m x 90cm/5ft x 3ft heavy artist's canvas
- staple gun (optional)
- white acrylic primer or matt emulsion (flat latex) paint
- medium decorator's paintbrush
- medium-grade abrasive paper
- ruler and pencil
- strong fabric adhesive
- metal spoon
- acetate sheet or stencil card
- craft knife and self-healing cutting mat
- spray mount
- artist's acrylics or stencil paints in blue, brick red, purple, light blue, dusky pink and light emerald green
- stencil brushes
- clear water-based varnish and brush
- small tubes of artist's acrylic paint in raw umber and raw sienna

1 Turn the canvas over. If you want to secure it, staple it down. Apply three coats of primer or emulsion (latex) paint, rubbing lightly with abrasive paper between coats.

2 Using a ruler and pencil, draw a border 4cm/1¹/₂in wide around the edge, mitring the corners. Apply strong fabric adhesive to the border and fold it flat, using the back of a spoon to apply pressure and smooth any bumps.

3 Mark out the design from the back of the book except for the stars. Paint the framework following the colour scheme illustrated.

▶

4 Cut three simple geometric stencils following the design at the back of the book from acetate sheet or stencil card using a sharp craft knife and self-healing cutting mat.

5 Stencil the red and blue stars in the centre of the large squares. Give the back of the stencil a light coat of spray mount to keep it in place as you paint. Use the paint sparingly on a dry brush but try to get a flat colour finish.

6 When the stars are dry add the purple and light blue triangles. Lightly spray the back of the stencil with adhesive and place it over the star, aligning the white space with the stencil cut-out.

7 The corner boxes are done in alternate colours. Begin by painting half of them using dusky pink acrylic or stencil paint and a medium-to-large stencil brush.

8 Finish the colour scheme for the floorcloth by painting the rest of the corner boxes with light emerald green acrylic or stencil paint.

9 Apply one coat of varnish tinted with a squeeze of raw umber and raw sienna acrylic paint to mellow the colour. Leave to dry then apply two coats of clear varnish, allowing adequate drying time between them.

STARS AND STRIPES FLOORCLOTH

Varnished floorcloths were introduced by the early American settlers, who recycled the canvas sails that had carried them to the New World. Make this bright floorcloth to cover most of the room or just as a small mat – artist's suppliers sell canvas in a wide range of sizes. It is available pre-primed or you can prime it yourself. Each coat of varnish you apply will add years to the floorcloth's life.

You will need

- natural-coloured artist's canvas, size as required
- ruler and pencil
- craft knife and self-healing cutting mat
- 5cm/2in double-sided carpet tape
- white acrylic primer (optional)
- medium decorator's brush
- masking tape
- acrylic paint in scarlet, cobalt blue and white
- tracing paper
- stencil card
- stencil brush
- clear or antique tinted matt (flat) polyurethane varnish and brush

1 Draw a 10cm/4in border on all four sides of the back of the canvas. Using a craft knife and cutting mat, cut across the corners as shown.

2 Stick double-sided carpet tape along the border line. Peel off the backing tape, then fold over the raw edge of the artist's canvas.

3 If the canvas is unprimed, apply two coats of white acrylic primer. Leave to dry.

4 Mark vertical stripes 7.5cm/3in wide down the canvas. Outline alternating stripes with masking tape.

5 Paint alternating stripes on the canvas with scarlet acrylic paint and a medium decorator's brush.

6 Leave to dry completely, then carefully peel off the low-tack masking tape.

7 Trace the star template at the back of the book. Cut out from stencil card using a craft knife and cutting mat.

8 Place the stencil on a white stripe, about 5cm/2in from one end of the canvas. Using a stencil brush, apply blue paint sparingly, working inwards from the points of the star. Wipe the back of the stencil to avoid smudging. Space the stars about 10cm/4in apart along all the white stripes.

9 Repeat with white acrylic paint stencilled on the red stripes, positioning the white stars to fall halfway between the blue stars.

10 Apply at least three coats of varnish, leaving to dry between coats. Use an antique tinted varnish if you wish to mellow the bright colours.

OPPOSITE: You can alter the colour of the stripes and the star motif to suit your preferences or your choice of flag.

HOME ACCESSORIES

Here is a selection of wonderful ideas that you can make for your own home or to give as a gift to mark a birthday or other special occasion. Picture frames, candles, vases and trays are indispensable items, which everybody needs to have, but they become exclusive accessories when embellished with stencilled designs. Etching fluid and gold leaf techniques add an air of exclusivity and are also interesting to do.

ABOVE: Cream church candles look stylish and fresh with the addition of a simple stencilled star motif.

LEFT: Glass etching spray is a simple method of creating the illusion of etched glass.

GILDED LAMPSHADE

A simple parchment lampshade makes an ideal base for gilding. The heraldic stencilled design on a shellac base coat gives the shade an antique appearance. Use a low-wattage bulb with this shade to avoid tarnishing.

You will need

- plain parchment lampshade
- stencil brushes
- amber shellac varnish
- tracing paper and pen
- stencil card or acetate
- craft knife and self-healing cutting mat
- masking tape
- gold stencil paint

1 Using a large round stencil brush, stipple an even but blotchy coat of amber shellac varnish over the surface of the lampshade. Leave to dry for 30 minutes to 1 hour.

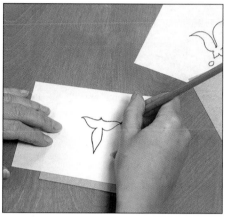

2 Trace the templates from the back of the book and transfer to stencil card or acetate.

3 Cut out the stencils using a craft knife and cutting mat.

4 Mark the positions for the stencils around the lampshade. Secure the first stencil at the bottom of the shade with masking tape. Stir the gold paint well, then stipple through the stencil. Do not load the brush with too much paint or it will bleed. Remove the stencil carefully before repositioning it.

5 When you have completed the bottom row, secure the second stencil at the top of the shade. Stencil the top row in the same way as before. Leave the shade to dry for at least 1 hour.

OPPOSITE: *You could try using silver, bronze or pewter stencil paint on this lampshade.*

ELIZABETHAN LAMPSHADE

Here, an Elizabethan border design is applied to a lampshade using a combination of sponge and stencil techniques. The pattern would also look sumptuous using deep blue or red with gold. For a larger lampshade, enlarge the template on a photocopier.

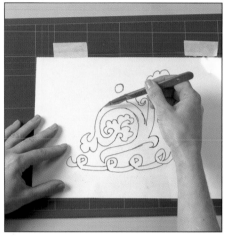

1 Trace the template at the back of the book on to the acetate sheet. Cut out using a craft knife and cutting mat or a heat knife.

2 Lay the design on a sheet of white paper and, using a stencil brush, apply undiluted black paint to the paper around the acetate. Keep the brush upright and dab, rather than brush, the paint on.

3 Apply the base colours of gold and white to the lampshade using a sponge. Take up only a small amount of paint each time, so that the texture of the sponge is transferred to the shade. Leave to dry.

4 Using strips of low-tack masking tape, attach the stencil to the lampshade. Use small curls of tape on the underside of the stencil to attach parts that do not lay flat.

5 Using the stencil brush, apply small amounts of black paint to the lampshade, gradually building up the density of colour. Remove the stencil and allow the paint to dry. To speed up the drying process, you can use a hairdryer.

6 Tape the stencil to the next position and apply paint as before until the whole lampshade has been patterned. Leave to dry.

7 Retape the stencil to the lampshade, taking care to position the stencil over the previous work. Use a small piece of sponge to apply gold highlights.

GOLD LEAF PICTURE FRAME

This picture frame has been decorated using a simple square stencil, which has been embellished with gold leaf. Applying leaf metals is a technique that should not be rushed.

1 Using a craft knife and a self-healing cutting mat, cut two pieces of card (stock) to the size that you wish your frame to be. Cut a central window in one piece. The frame illustrated here has a total area of 21 x 21cm/8$^{1}/_{2}$ x 8$^{1}/_{2}$in with a central window of 9 x 9cm/3$^{1}/_{2}$ x 3$^{1}/_{2}$in.

2 Cut out a piece of canvas, linen or heavy silk 2cm/$^{3}/_{4}$in larger all around than the picture frame.

3 Apply spray mount to the frame and place it in the centre of the fabric, wrong side up. Rub your hand over the card to form a secure bond.

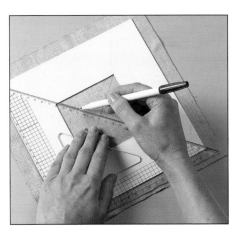

4 Using a vanishing fabric pen or pencil, draw two diagonals across the window. Measure and cut out a 5cm/2in square in the centre of the frame.

5 Apply strips of double-sided tape all round the reverse edges of the frame. Pull the extra fabric back and stick it down. Cut a mitre in each corner and stitch.

▶

6 To keep the back of the frame neat and tidy, apply masking tape over the raw edges of the fabric.

7 Using a craft knife, cut a piece of stencil card or acetate film to a rectangle the same size as one side of the frame, corner to corner (21 x 6cm/8½ x 2½in for the frame illustrated). Mark out equally spaced squares along the length (4cm/1½in squares with a 1cm/½in division), and cut out.

8 Using masking tape, attach the stencil to one side of the front of the frame. Fill in the squares with colour using a stencil brush or sponge. Leave to dry then remove the stencil and tape it to the next side, matching the corner squares. Continue until all four sides have been coloured.

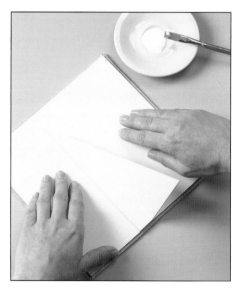

9 Carefully following the manufacturer's instructions, apply a small gold leaf square inside the stencilled one. Usually, this involves applying size and leaving for 15 minutes before applying the gold leaf with a soft brush. Leave for about 2 hours to set, then buff up the gold leaf and remove the unstuck pieces of gold.

10 Using heavy card and a sharp-bladed craft knife, cut out a right-angled triangle of the same height as the frame and 10cm/4in wide. Score along the longest side 1cm/½in from the edge and then use PVA (white) glue to stick it to the backing board cut out in step 1.

11 Apply PVA glue to the reverse of the backing board on three sides and stick it to the frame. The top is left open to slide in a picture. To protect the gold leaf and to prevent dust from collecting on the fabric, paint the front of the frame with one or two coats of clear varnish or lacquer.

FRAMED CHALKBOARD

Once you have had a chalkboard in the kitchen it becomes one of life's absolute essentials. Here the frame is made of an old plank sawn into four pieces – two long, two short glued together. Choose the size to suit your wall space. Cramp the frame while the glue sets or hold it together with string, twisting a pencil in the string to tighten it.

You will need

- frame made up as above
- tracing paper and pen
- spray mount
- stencil card
- craft knife and self-healing cutting mat
- emulsion (latex) paints in dull blue and red
- small decorator's paintbrush
- medium-grade abrasive paper
- spray mount
- stencil brush
- artist's acrylic paint in black
- antiquing varnish and brush
- hardboard, 2.5cm/1in larger all around than the inner frame measurement
- blackboard paint
- small hammer and panel pins (brads)
- (you will also need a piece of chalk!)

1 Trace the templates, or enlarge them on a photocopier. Spray the back lightly with spray mount and stick on to stencil card. Cut out the shapes using a craft knife and cutting mat.

2 Paint the frame with dull blue emulsion (latex) paint. Leave to dry completely.

3 Paint the inner and outer edges of the frame with red emulsion paint. Leave to dry.

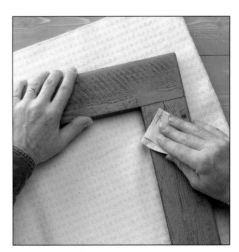

4 Rub the paint with medium-grade abrasive paper to reveal the grain of the wood.

5 Spray the back of each stencil lightly with spray mount and position on the frame. Arrange the shapes as shown in the main picture.

6 Using a small stencil brush, lightly apply the red emulsion paint to the frame.

7 Darken the red paint slightly by mixing in a little black acrylic paint.

8 Using the stencil brush, rub the dark red paint deep into the grain in just a few places.

9 When dry, rub over with abrasive paper to remove any dark red paint from the surface.

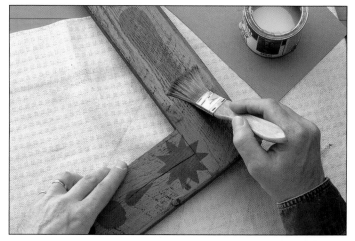

10 Apply one or two coats of antiquing varnish. Leave the frame to dry.

OPPOSITE: *The best country accessories usually look worn and loved like this framed chalkboard.*

11 Paint the hardboard with two coats of blackboard paint. Leave to dry.

12 Attach the blackboard to the back of the frame, using panel pins (brads).

LEAFY PICTURE FRAMES

The stylish raised leaf patterns around these frames are simple to create using ordinary white interior filler instead of paint to fill in the stencilled leaf shapes. The simple shapes can be cut out with scissors.

You will need

- 2 wooden frames
- dark green acrylic paint
- medium decorator's paintbrush
- fine-grade abrasive paper
- stencil card
- scissors
- ready-mixed interior filler
- stencil brush

1 Paint the frames dark green. When dry, gently rub them down with abrasive paper to create a subtle distressed effect.

2 Enlarge the templates at the back of the book to fit the frames. Transfer the designs to stencil card and cut them out using scissors.

3 Position a stencil on the first frame and stipple ready-mixed filler through the stencil. Reposition the stencil and continue all around the frame. Leave to dry.

4 Repeat with a different combination of motifs on the second frame. When the filler is completely hard, gently smooth over the leaves with abrasive paper.

OPPOSITE: You can also use textured gel combined with acrylic paint and stippled on to the frame to achieve a similar effect.

ART NOUVEAU HATBOX

An elegantly stencilled hatbox and matching shoe bag would be perfect for storing a bride's hat and shoes. Make a set for yourself or to give to someone special. And you needn't stop there: stencil a whole stack of matching hatboxes to use for stylish storage in a bedroom.

You will need

- round hatbox
- medium decorator's paintbrushes
- white undercoat
- pale green water-based woodwash
- tape measure
- pencil
- tracing paper and pen
- stencil card
- craft knife and self-healing cutting mat
- ruler
- spray mount
- stencil brushes
- stencil paints in dark green, royal blue and pale green

1 Paint the hatbox with two coats of white undercoat. Dilute one part pale green woodwash with one part water and apply two or three light washes to the hatbox, allowing them to dry between coats. Measure the circumference of the box and divide by six or eight. Lightly mark the measurements on the lid and side of the box with a pencil.

2 Trace the flower and heart templates at the back of the book and cut from stencil card. Rule a pencil line across the bottom of the stencil to help align it on the box. Spray with spray mount and position on the box. Using a stencil brush and dark green stencil paint, stencil the leaves and stem. Remove the stencil when dry, respray with spray mount and reposition.

3 Continue to work around the box. Reposition the stencil on the leaves and add shadow to the points where the leaves join the stem, using royal blue paint and a clean brush.

LEFT: Stencil a matching calico shoe bag to protect a treasured pair of shoes.

OPPOSITE: Line a hatbox with matching tissue paper.

4 Using the single heart stencil, add a pale green heart between each pair of leaves.

5 Stencil flowerheads around the rim of the lid in dark green, adding a royal blue shadow as before. Stencil the flower motif in the centre of the lid.

6 Add pale green heart motifs around the main motif, using a very small amount of paint for a delicate touch.

CITRUS FRUIT TRAY

This bamboo tray has been given a tropical look with juicy orange and lime stencils, perfect for summer drinks on a sunny day. You could also transform an old tray by painting over the existing surface.

1 Sand the tray lightly to remove any existing varnish. Trace the templates at the back of the book and tape on to stencil card. Using a craft knife and cutting mat cut them out, leaving a narrow margin round each motif.

2 Stipple a couple of pale orange circles using a small to medium-size stencil brush, as the background for the orange slices, protecting the surface of the rest of the tray with masking tape.

3 Fix the circle stencil back in place over the oranges and slot the segment stencil within it. Using dark orange, fill in the segments, adding some light and dark stippling to create texture within the shapes.

4 Stipple the lime and leaves in two shades of green. Give the fruit a more three-dimensional look by stippling light green in the centre and dark green around the outside edge. Stipple the stalk in dark brown.

5 Stencil the "rind" of the lime segments in dark green and the main part in light green. Add light white stippling across the "pips". Leave to dry completely then apply three coats of gloss or matt (flat) varnish.

GILDED CANDLES

Church candles look extra special adorned with simple gold stars and stripes. Always associated with Christmas, candles are popular all year round for their soft romantic lighting. Cutting the stencils may be fiddly but it is then a quick job to spray on the gold paint.

You will need

- acetate
- selection of candles
- marker pen
- tracing paper and pen
- craft knife and self-healing cutting mat
- spray mount
- masking tape
- metallic spray paint
- protective face mask

1 Wrap a piece of acetate around the candle. Mark and cut it to fit exactly. Do not overlap the edges. Cut it a few millimetres shorter than the candle.

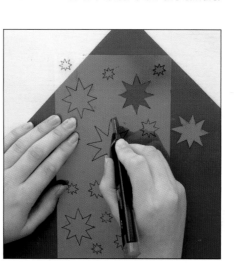

2 Trace the star templates at the back of the book. Lay a piece of acetate over the stars and trace over them with a marker pen.

3 Cut out the stars using a craft knife and cutting mat.

4 Spray one side of the stencil with spray mount and wrap around the candle, centring it so that there is a small gap at either end. Secure the acetate join with masking tape. Mask the top of the candle, ensuring there are no gaps.

RIGHT: Create a range of attractive gilded patterns by varying the size of the stencilled stars and stripes used on the candles.

5 Spray a very fine mist of metallic spray paint over the candle, holding the can about 30cm/12in from the surface. If too much paint is applied, it will drip underneath the stencil. Keep checking that the stencil is well stuck down to avoid any fuzzy lines around the stars. Leave the paint to dry for a couple of minutes, then carefully remove the masking tape and acetate.

6 For a stars and stripes candle, cut strips of acetate and trace a line of stars along each strip. Cut out as before. Spray one side of the acetate strips with spray mount. Stick the strips on to the candle at equal spaces. Secure them with small pieces of tape at the join.

7 Mask off the top of the candle as before. Spray the candle with metallic paint and remove the masking tape and stencil when dry.

8 For a reverse stencil design, cut out individual star shapes from acetate. Apply spray mount to one side, stick on to the candle and mask off the top of the candle as before. Spray with metallic paint and carefully remove the acetate stars when the paint is dry.

CITRUS FRUIT BOWL

Stencilling offers a quick and easy method of decorating china and this lime motif is ideal for a fruit bowl. The simple shape of the lime can be drawn freehand.

You will need

- soft pencil
- tracing paper
- masking tape
- stencil card
- craft knife and self-healing cutting mat
- plain china bowl
- cleaning fluid
- clean cotton rag
- yellow chinagraph pencil
- water-based ceramic paints in citrus green, mid-green, dark green and yellow
- artist's paintbrushes
- acrylic varnish and brush (optional)

1 Draw a freehand lime shape on tracing paper. Using masking tape to hold the tracing paper in place, transfer the outline to a piece of stencil card. Cut all around the shape using a craft knife and cutting mat.

2 Clean the china bowl. Attach the stencil to the bowl using masking tape. Draw inside the stencil outline on to the bowl using a yellow chinagraph pencil. Repeat the lime motif all over the bowl.

3 Fill in all the lime shapes with citrus green paint using a fine artist's brush. Leave the paint to dry completely then add highlights to each of the fruits, using the mid-green paint. Leave the paint to dry.

4 Paint a stalk at the end of each lime shape in dark green paint. Leave to dry. Paint the background all over the outside of the bowl yellow, leaving a thin white outline around each of the lime shapes to help them stand out.

5 Apply a coat of acrylic varnish over the painted section, or bake the bowl in the oven following the paint manufacturer's instructions.

LEAF-ETCHED VASE

The delicate effect of etched glass is easy to imitate nowadays with a glass etching spray, which is now available from most good art and craft suppliers. For the best results, spray through a stencil cut from adhesive plastic.

You will need

- tracing paper and pen
- masking tape
- sticky-back plastic (contact paper)
- craft knife and self-healing cutting mat
- straight-sided vase at least 23cm/9in tall
- object taller than the vase to support it while spraying
- glass etching spray
- scrap piece of plastic or paper

1 Trace the template at the back of the book. Using masking tape, tape the tracing face down on to the back of a piece of sticky-back plastic (contact paper). Draw over the design to transfer it. Cut out the stencil using a craft knife and cutting mat.

2 Make sure the vase is clean and free from grease. Trim the tracing to fit inside the vase. Tape the tracing inside the front of the vase. Peel the backing paper off the stencils and stick in position on the front of the vase matching the positions on the template.

3 Upturn the vase and slip it over a taller item so the vase rim does not rest on the work surface. Cover the surrounding area with a scrap piece of plastic or paper. Spray the vase with glass etching spray following the manufacturer's instructions.

4 Leave the vase to dry thoroughly and apply a second coat if necessary. Carefully peel off all the stencils. Do not clean the vase in a dishwasher but wash gently in warm soapy water.

STATIONERY
AND PAPER

S tencilling on to paper is easy, quick and fun and any good art store or stationer should have a selection of handmade and textured papers to choose from. You can make lanterns, greetings cards, gift tags or wedding stationery, or stencil a whole sheet of paper to wrap up a present or cover a special book. Ready-made boxes can also be adorned with patterns to turn them into special storage containers for keepsakes and gifts.

ABOVE: Paper lanterns with various stencilled motifs can be used to decorate a room during a festive season.

LEFT: Handmade stencilled Christmas wrapping paper will add a special touch to any present.

TAURUS GIFT WRAP

Personalize a special birthday gift for a friend or loved one with gift wrap stencilled with their relevant star sign. Deep red and black have been used here to match the energetic, earthy character of the Taurean but you can choose colours to suit the person.

You will need

- thin card (stock) or paper and pencil
- acetate sheet
- black felt-tipped pen
- craft knife and self-healing cutting mat
- plain deep red gift wrap
- masking tape
- black acrylic paint
- stencil brush

1 Using the main photograph as a guide, draw the Taurus motif freehand on to card (stock) or paper.

2 Place the acetate over the template and trace the outline with a black felt-tipped pen. Cut out the stencil using a craft knife and cutting mat.

3 Decide on the positioning of the motifs on the gift wrap, marking lightly with a pencil if necessary. Position the stencil and use a little masking tape to hold it in place. Stipple the design with the stencil brush. Lift the stencil off carefully and repeat to cover the paper.

BUTTERFLY GIFT WRAP

Original hand-printed wrapping paper turns a present into something very special. Once you've tried stencilling you may never want to buy printed gift wrap again.

You will need

- tracing paper and pen
- acetate sheet
- black felt-tipped pen
- craft knife and self-healing cutting mat
- coloured paper
- masking paper
- stencil brush
- acrylic paints in red and black

1 Trace the butterfly template at the back of the book, enlarging it on a photocopier if necessary. Place a piece of acetate over it and draw the wings for the first stencil, using a felt-tipped pen. Use a second piece of acetate to make a stencil of the body and wing markings.

2 Cut out both stencils using a craft knife and cutting mat. Secure the first stencil lightly to the paper with masking tape and then stipple on the red paint. Do not overload the stencil brush. Reposition the acetate stencil and repeat to cover the paper.

3 When the red acrylic paint is completely dry, secure the second butterfly stencil in place with masking tape. Stipple on the black paint and then repeat to complete all the butterflies. You can try this in different colourways.

SEAWEED GIFT WRAP

Swirling seaweed shapes in shades of green and blue produce an underwater effect that makes a really unusual wrapping paper. Vary the paint colours according to the background paper you choose.

You will need

- tracing paper and pen
- black felt-tipped pen
- acetate sheet
- craft knife and self-healing cutting mat
- blue-green wrapping paper
- acrylic paints in sap green, white and blue
- stencil brushes

1 Trace the templates A, B and C from the back of the book, enlarging them on a photocopier if necessary. Go over the outline with the black pen. Lay the acetate on top and cut out the stencil using a craft knife and cutting mat.

2 Position the acetate stencil on the wrapping paper. Mix sap green acrylic paint with a little white paint. Using a stencil brush, stencil templates A and B side by side in rows across the paper, leaving space for a row of template C between them.

3 Using white paint, add highlights to the seaweed tips.

4 Mix blue paint with white and stencil C in rows, leaving a stencil space in between for the lighter blue seaweeds. Overlap some of the fronds slightly.

SNOWFLAKE GIFT WRAP

Create your own Christmas gift wrap and your friends and family will appreciate their presents even more than usual. This is one project where the finished effect is more important than accuracy and neatness, so it is quicker than you might think.

1 Trace the three templates at the back of the book and tape on to stencil card. Using a craft knife and cutting mat, cut each one out in a single piece. The cut-out shapes will be used to make a reverse stencil.

2 Load the stencil brush with white paint. Using the first stencil, block in a scattering of positive snowflakes across the sheet of wrapping paper. Leave enough space between them to fit in the other motifs, about six or seven shapes.

3 Fill in some of the spaces between them with positive stencils of the other two snowflake stencils, overlapping them if you wish.

4 To make reverse stencils of the three snowflakes, use a blocking action to work over the outlines and on to the surrounding background.

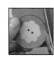

BUTTON GIFT WRAP AND GIFT TAGS

Stencil colourful button motifs at random on plain paper to make an unusual gift wrap, with cut-out buttons as co-ordinating gift tags.

You will need

- tracing paper and pen
- masking tape
- stencil card
- craft knife and self-healing cutting mat
- white paper
- soft pencil
- acrylic paints in pink, mustard, lilac, turquoise and dark green
- ceramic tile
- flat paintbrush
- stencil brush
- eraser
- coloured card (stock)
- scissors
- hole punch

1 Trace the template at the back of the book. Tape a piece of stencil card to the tracings with masking tape. Cut out the stencils using a craft knife and cutting mat. You will need three stencils – the outer buttons and heart button, the inner buttons, and the buttonholes. Tape the outer button and heart button stencil to white paper with masking tape, then mark the registration marks lightly with a soft pencil.

2 Apply a thin coat of pink paint to a ceramic tile with the flat paintbrush. Dab at the paint with a stencil brush and stencil a button holding the stencil brush upright and moving it in a circular motion. Stencil all the buttons using pink, mustard, lilac and turquoise acrylic paint. Leave to dry completely.

3 Remove the stencil. Tape the inner button stencil in place, matching the registration marks. Stencil the inner buttons, using colours that contrast with the outer buttons. Leave to dry.

4 Remove the stencil. Tape the button-hole stencil in place, matching the marks. Stencil the buttonholes using dark green paint. Remove the stencil and erase the marks. Tape the outer button stencil to the paper in a different position. Continue until the paper is covered. ▶

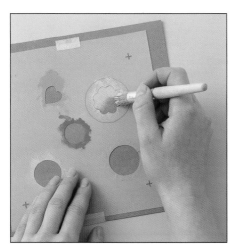

5 To make a button gift tag, draw a 5cm/2in diameter circle on coloured card. Tape the outer button stencil of the flower-shaped button in the centre. Mark the registration marks. Stencil the button. Leave to dry. Remove the stencil.

6 Tape the buttonhole stencil in place, matching up the registration marks. Stencil the buttonholes in dark green acrylic paint. Leave to dry completely then cut out the circle with sharp scissors.

7 Punch a hole at one edge of the tag using a hole punch. Tie up the parcel using co-ordinating coloured wool, thread or string and threading it through the button gift tag to secure in place.

BUTTERFLY GREETINGS CARDS

The simple outlines of these three butterflies can be used in various combinations to produce a range of very personal greetings cards. Here are just a few ideas of how they could be used – the possibilities are endless.

You will need

◆ selection of handmade paper, tracing paper and blank cards in pinks, lilacs and purples
◆ tracing paper and pen or carbon paper and sharp pencil
◆ masking tape
◆ stencil card
◆ craft knife and self-healing cutting mat
◆ acrylic paints in pink, purple and lilac
◆ stencil brush
◆ PVA (white) glue
◆ ruler

1 Trace the templates at the back of the book and tape on to stencil card. Cut out, using a craft knife and cutting mat. Stencil a single pink butterfly on to a small rectangle of textured handmade paper. Cut four angled slots in a purple card blank to mount it, one at each corner, and slip the paper in place under the slots.

2 For a card with a three-dimensional look, stencil several overlapping butterflies on to a paper blank, each in a different colour. Cut out carefully around the edges of the wings with a craft knife. Ease the wings gently upwards so that the butterflies appear to be in flight but do not cut into the central bodies.

3 Create a multi-layered image by stencilling four butterflies on to a piece of tracing paper. Stencil more butterflies on to the front of a darker card blank. Trim the trace to size and glue it to the front of the card.

4 If your paper does not have a deckle edge, tearing it against a ruler will give an attractive finish to the card. Mount the finished piece as in step 1 to make a larger version of the single butterfly card.

▶

WEDDING STATIONERY

Linked rings are a symbol of love because they have no end, so these elegantly entwined rings and hearts are ideal motifs for wedding stationery. Continue the theme and stencil them on invitations, place names and thank you cards.

1 Trace the templates at the back of the book. Place a piece of carbon paper face down on to stencil card and tape the tracing on top. Redraw the template with a sharp pencil to transfer the design. Using a craft knife and cutting mat, cut out the stencil.

2 Tape the linked rings stencil to the top of a sheet of writing paper either in a corner or centrally. Using a flat paintbrush, spread a thin coat of gold paint on to a ceramic tile. Dab at the paint with a stencil brush and stencil the rings.

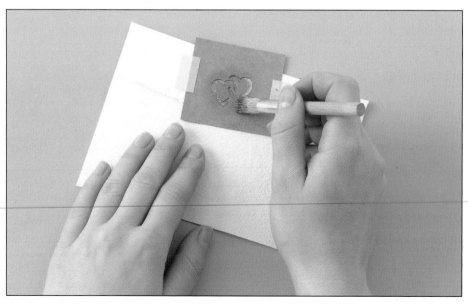

3 Stencil the linked hearts centrally on the back flap of an envelope. Leave the stationery to dry. The stencils can be used in various ways, the linked rings on the envelope or the linked hearts in a row as a border on an invitation or on writing paper for example.

HANDPRINTED BOOK COVERS

These small overall repeat prints are inspired by the individual woodcut patterns that appeared on hand-bound books of the past. Stencil several sheets, using a different colour for each volume or book title.

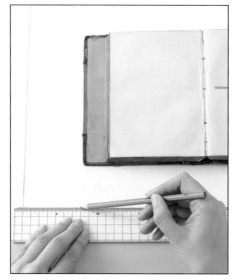

1 Measure the width of the book from the edge of the back cover to the edge of the front cover (including the spine), and its height. Add on 10cm/4in to each measurement to allow for the folded turnings. Draw a horizontal rectangle on the paper to this size.

2 Trace the template at the back of the book and tape on to stencil card. Cut out, using a craft knife and cutting mat. Starting at the right side edge and using only a small amount of paint on the brush, stencil in the first block of pattern.

3 To continue the repeat, line up the right edge of the stencil with the completed print. Line up the pattern by eye, so that the painted areas can be seen within the cut-out shapes. Continue filling in blocks of pattern to fill in the entire rectangle. Use an extra piece of paper where necessary to protect the stencilled area. Leave the stencilled paper to dry completely.

OPPOSITE: Stencilled bookcovers can give a new lease of life to a book and look good on bookshelves.

4 Cut out the cover and wrap it around the book to find out where the spine fits. Cut slanting lines in to each edge of the spine and fold over the side and top and bottom edges.

5 Unfold the four edges, mitre the corners by turning them in at 45-degree angles. Refold the edges to check that the cover will fit when the book is closed, and adjust them if necessary.

6 Put the jacket back over the book and fold the edges back in place. Secure each corner with a light dab of glue. For a different look, stencil in white on a coloured background.

CONFETTI BOX

Make a pretty box ready for scattering confetti at a wedding and stencil it with a romantic pair of cupid's wings. You can put wedding keepsakes in it afterwards.

You will need

- pen
- bright blue card (stock)
- craft knife and self-healing cutting mat
- metal ruler
- scissors
- tracing paper
- carbon paper
- masking tape
- stencil card
- sharp pencil
- silver acrylic paint
- ceramic tile
- small flat decorator's paintbrush
- stencil brush
- double-sided adhesive tape

1 Referring to the templates at the back of the book, draw the box and lid on bright blue card (stock). Using a craft knife and cutting mat, cut out the box and lid plus an 11.7cm/4⅝in square for the base, cutting the straight edges against a metal ruler. Score the box and lid along the broken lines with the blade of a pair of scissors against the ruler.

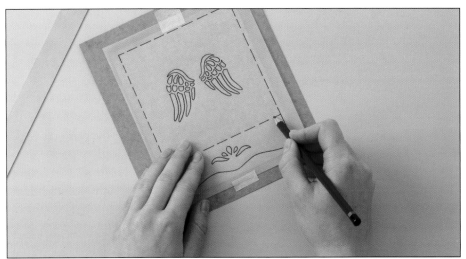

2 Trace the lid template on to tracing paper with a pen, tracing the top of the lid and one side edge. Place a piece of carbon paper face down on a piece of stencil card. Tape the tracing on top with masking tape. Redraw the template with a sharp pencil to transfer the design. Remove the template. Cut out the wings and the border motif using a craft knife and cutting mat.

▶

3 Tape the stencil to the lid with masking tape. Apply a thin coat of silver paint to a ceramic tile with the paintbrush. Dab at the paint with a stencil brush and stencil the wings.

4 Stencil the border motif. Leave the paint to dry then move the stencil around the lid to stencil the next side edge. Stencil all the side edges. Leave to dry.

5 Apply double-sided tape to the end tab of the box on the right side. Apply double-sided tape to the base tabs of the box and the tabs of the lid on the wrong side. Fold the box and lid backwards along the scored lines.

6 Wrap the box around the base and stick the base tabs under the base folding the scored edges of the box around the corners of the base.

7 Stick the end tab inside the opposite end of the box. Run your fingers along the joins to secure the tabs in place.

8 Firmly stick the tabs on the lid under the adjacent ends of the side edges.

PASTEL PAPER LANTERNS

Suspend these pretty lanterns by their handles on colourful ribbons or omit the handles and slip them over a night-light. The candle glow will softly illuminate the translucent paper. Never leave naked flames unattended.

You will need

- tracing paper and pen
- transfer paper
- stencil card
- masking tape
- sharp pencil
- craft knife and self-healing cutting mat
- metal ruler
- scissors
- translucent paper in mauve, pale blue and purple
- acrylic paint in lavender and grey
- ceramic tile
- small flat decorator's paintbrush
- stencil brush
- double-sided adhesive tape

1 Trace the template at the back of the book. Place a piece of transfer paper face down on a piece of stencil card. Tape the tracing on top with masking tape. Redraw the template with a sharp pencil to transfer the design. Cut out the stencil using a craft knife and cutting mat.

2 Using the craft knife and cutting mat, cut a 23 x 13cm/9 x 5in rectangle of mauve translucent paper for the lantern. Tape the stencil centrally on top. Apply a thin coat of lavender paint to a ceramic tile. Dab at the paint with a stencil brush and stencil the feather holding the stencil brush upright, moving it in a circular motion.

3 Leave to dry then blend the grey and lavender paint together. Stencil in the tips of the feather.

4 Cut strips of double-sided tape 5mm/¼in wide. Apply one strip to one short edge of the lantern. Peel off the backing tape. Overlap the short ends and stick them together.

5 Using the craft knife and cutting mat, cut a 23.5 x 2.5cm/9¼ x 1in strip of pale blue translucent paper. Apply a strip of 5mm/¼in wide double-sided tape to one long edge. Cut a fringe 2mm/¹⁄₁₂in wide to the tape.

6 Peel off the backing part of the double-sided tape and stick down the fringe around the top of the lantern keeping the upper edges level and overlapping the ends of the fringe at the back.

7 Cut a 22 x 1.5cm/8¾ x ⅝in strip of purple paper for the handle. Centre the feather and stick the ends of the handle inside the top of the lantern at each side with double-sided tape.

RIGHT: These translucent pastel paper lanterns will add a special touch to any festive party. They can be hung both inside and outdoors.

SHOE BOX

Flat-pack boxes are easy to decorate before assembly. These glamorous high-heeled stencilled shoes will transform a utilitarian cardboard box into a storage container worthy of your favourite footwear.

You will need

- tracing paper and pen or carbon paper and sharp pencil
- masking tape
- stencil card
- craft knife and self-healing cutting mat
- flat-pack storage box
- acrylic paints in silver, turquoise and dark green
- stencil brush

1 Trace the templates at the back of the book and tape on to stencil card. Cut out using a craft knife and cutting mat. Decide where the first shoe is to go. Using silver paint and a dry brush, stipple in the drop shadow using the bottom half of the stencil.

2 Position the stencil slightly upwards and to the left of the shadow so that the bottom part of the shadow is covered. Fill in the entire shoe using a small stencil brush and turquoise paint. Use two layers if necessary to cover up all the silver paint.

3 Continue stencilling shoes at intervals over the box and lid, varying the angles and alternating between the three different stencils. Add a dark green bow to the front of some of the shoes.

4 When the paint is quite dry, assemble the box, following the instructions supplied by the manufacturer. Line the box with matching tissue paper as a luxurious finishing touch, and to protect your shoes.

TEMPLATES

The templates on the following pages may be resized to any scale required. The simplest way of doing this is to enlarge them on a photocopier, or trace the design and draw a grid of evenly spaced squares over your tracing. Draw a larger grid on another piece of paper and copy the outline square by square. Draw over the lines to make sure they are continuous.

GREEK URNS
page 32

MAKING SANDCASTLES
page 78

FLAG STENCILS
page 80

FOLK ART WALL
page 54

TROMPE L'OEIL PLATES
page 34

PENNSYLVANIA DUTCH TULIPS
page 56

LEAFY FIREPLACE
SURROUND
page 63

ELEGANT ROSE
TREE
page 66

PAISLEY
PATTERN
WALL
page 60

GREEK KEY FLOOR
BORDER
page 100

VICTORIAN WINDOW
page 94

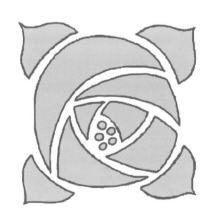

ART NOUVEAU TILES
page 96

MEDALLION
STENCILLED FLOOR
page 98

FRENCH COUNTRY
KITCHEN
page 42

BRIGHT TRANSPORT
BORDER
page 90

RENAISSANCE
HALLWAY
page 51

STAR BATHROOM
page 73

HERALDIC DINING ROOM
page 45

KITCHEN ALCOVE
page 38

**CHILD'S SEASIDE
ROOM**
page 82

CLASSICAL URN PANELS
page 48

ANIMAL BEDROOM
page 86

**JAPANESE ORANGE
BLOSSOM WALL**
page 70

BRONZE CHAIR *page 104*

BATHROOM
FRIEZE
page 76

HAWAIIAN HIBISCUS
CABINET
page 116

SCANDINAVIAN CHAIR *page 107*

PAINTED DRAWERS *page 110*

ELIZABETHAN
LAMPSHADE
page 196

TRAIN TOY
BOX
page 113

CELTIC
KNOT BOX
page 120

DAISY STOOL
page 123

GILDED
LAMPSHADE
page 194

STRIPED TABLE
AND CHAIRS
page 132

ORGANZA
CUSHION
page 140

AFRICAN BEDSIDE CHEST *page 129*

CITRUS ROLLER BLIND
page 154

FLOWER POWER CHAIR
page 136

FIFTIES
ROSE
CUSHIONS
page 142

SPRIGGED CURTAIN
page 150

ZODIAC CAFE CURTAIN
page 152

DRAGONFLY CURTAIN
page 145

RAINFOREST CURTAINS
page 145

MOSAIC TABLECLOTH
page 160

GARDEN SHADOWS BLIND
page 156

ROSE TABLECLOTH
page 164

AEOLMRUV

LOVE PILLOWS
page 172

FEATHER
THROW
page 169

SEASHELL
BEACH
BAG
page 178

SUMMER QUILT
COVER
page 166

GIRL'S BED CANOPY
AND CUSHION
page 174

GINGERBREAD APRON
page 180

SEVENTIES FLOWER CANVASES
page 183

**STARS AND STRIPES
FLOORCLOTH**
page 189

AMISH FLOORCLOTH
page 186

**FRAMED
CHALKBOARD**
page 201

**CITRUS
FRUIT TRAY**
page 208

**ART
NOUVEAU
HATBOX**
page 206

GILDED
CANDLES
page 210

LEAF-ETCHED VASE
page 214

LEAFY PICTURE FRAMES
page 204

CONFETTI
BOX
page 232

BUTTERFLY GREETINGS CARDS
page 226

SEAWEED GIFT WRAP
page 220

**SNOWFLAKE
GIFT WRAP**
page 222

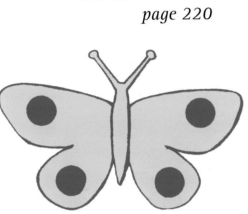

BUTTERFLY GIFT WRAP
page 219

**BUTTON GIFT WRAP
AND TAGS**
page 224

HANDPRINTED BOOK COVERS
page 230

**WEDDING
STATIONERY**
page 228

PASTEL PAPER LANTERNS
page 235

SHOE BOX
page 238

INDEX

ACKNOWLEDGEMENTS

The projects were created by Lucinda Ganderton, with the following exceptions:

Petra Boase: Making sandcastles (pp. 78–9), Painted drawers (pp. 110–12), Leafy picture frames (pp. 204–5).
Penny Boylan: Citrus roller blind (pp. 154–5).
Sacha Cohen: Greek urns (pp. 32–3), Heraldic dining room (pp. 45–7).
Emma Hardy: Trompe l'oeil plates (pp. 34–7), Organza cushion (pp. 140–1), Gilded candles (pp. 210–11).
Alison Jenkins: Rainforest curtains (pp. 147–9), Mosaic tablecloth (pp. 160–3).
Cheryl Owen: Kitchen alcove (pp. 38–41), Classical urn panels (pp. 48–50), Elegant rose wall (pp. 66–9), Bathroom frieze (pp. 76–7), Child's seaside room (pp. 82–5), Bright transport border (pp. 90–3), Scandinavian chair (pp. 107–9), Train toy box (pp. 113–15), Hawaiian hibiscus cabinet (pp. 116–19), Daisy stool (pp. 123–5), African bedside chest (pp. 129–31), Striped table and chairs (pp. 132–5), Dragonfly curtain (pp. 144–6), Girl's bed canopy and cushion (pp. 174–7), Leaf-etched vase (pp. 214–5), Button gift wrap and gift tags (pp. 224–5), Wedding stationery (pp. 228–9), Confetti box (pp. 232–4), Pastel paper lanterns (pp. 235–7).
Sandra Partington: Elizabethan lampshade (pp. 196–7).
Marie Perkins: Citrus fruit bowl (pp. 212–13).
Judy Smith: Flag stencils (pp. 80–1).
Suzie Stokoe: Summer quilt cover (pp. 164–6), Gold leaf picture frame (pp. 198–200).
Liz Wagstaff: Gilded lampshade (pp. 194–5).
Stewart and Sally Walton: Folk art wall (pp. 54–5), Star bathroom (pp. 73–5), Animal bedroom (pp. 86–9), Victorian window (pp. 49–5), Medallion stencilled floor (pp. 98–9), Bronze chair (pp. 104–5), Love pillows (pp. 172–3), Amish floorcloth (pp.186–8), Stars and stripes floorcloth (pp. 189–91), Framed chalkboard (pp. 201–3).
Josephine Whitfield: Taurus gift wrap (p. 218), Butterfly gift wrap (p. 219), Seaweed gift wrap (pp. 220–1).